ᴗ bʏ

Teaching Able, Gifted and Talented Children

Education at SAGE

SAGE is a leading international publisher of journals, books, and electronic media for academic, educational, and professional markets.

Our education publishing includes:

- accessible and comprehensive texts for aspiring education professionals and practitioners looking to further their careers through continuing professional development

- inspirational advice and guidance for the classroom

- authoritative state of the art reference from the leading authors in the field

Find out more at: **www.sagepub.co.uk/education**

Teaching Able, Gifted and Talented Children

Strategies, Activities and Resources

Clive Tunnicliffe

Los Angeles | London | New Delhi
Singapore | Washington DC

© Clive Tunnicliffe 2010

Apart from any fair dealing for the purposes of research or private
study, or criticism or review, as permitted under the Copyright,
Designs and Patents Act, 1988, this publication may be
reproduced, stored or transmitted in any form, or by any means,
only with the prior permission in writing of the publishers, or in
the case of reprographic reproduction, in accordance with the
terms of licences issued by the Copyright Licensing Agency.
Enquiries concerning reproduction outside those terms should be
sent to the publishers.

SAGE Publications Ltd
1 Oliver's Yard
55 City Road
London EC1Y 1SP

SAGE Publications Inc
2455 Teller Road
Thousand Oaks, California 91320

SAGE Publications India Pvt Ltd
B 1/I 1 Mohan Cooperative Industrial Area
Mathura Road
New Delhi 110 044

SAGE Publications Asia-Pacific Pte Ltd
33 Pekin Street #02–01
Far East Square
Singapore 048763

Library of Congress Control Number: 2009937142

British Library Cataloguing in Publication data
A catalogue record for this book is available from the British Library

ISBN 978-1-4129-4766-4
ISBN 978-1-4129-4767-1 (pbk)

Typeset by Dorwyn, Wells, Somerset
Printed in Great Britain by CPI Antony Rowe, Chippenham, Wiltshire
Printed on paper from sustainable resources

FSC
www.fsc.org
MIX
Paper from
responsible sources
FSC® C013604

Contents

Acknowledgements

I would like to thank Jude Bowen and Amy Jarrold of Sage Publications for their unfailing support throughout the writing of this book. This expression of appreciation is more than the conventional vote of thanks for editorial assistance. It is in no small part due to their good humour, patience and professionalism that the text in its present form has come to publication and I owe them a genuine debt of gratitude for that.

I would also like to thank my wife Patricia for the advice and support she gave me in seeing this project to completion. I could not have done it without her.

About the author

Dr Clive Tunnicliffe has wide and successful experience as a teacher, adviser, trainer, inspector and manager. He first became a Local Authority adviser for gifted and talented children in 1990, a post he held for five years. From this post he moved to another authority where he performed a number of roles, including English inspector, national strategy manager in the primary and secondary phases and, eventually, senior manager leading on audit and organizational review. He has been a successful academic (completing a PhD in Shakespearean studies as a major state scholarship holder, and also an MA in Language and Literature in Education) and for a number of years was a senior A level examiner and moderator. He has also enjoyed great success as a trainer with a broad range of educational experience and interests, particularly relating to learning and creativity.

Clive's work has covered all phases of the maintained sector from early years through to Further Education provision. He recently led an education, leisure and libraries department through its Ofsted inspection and the Annual Performance Assessment (APA) of Children's Services (being named employee of the year in the process). This focus on organizational audit and self-review led him to work as a member of a national steering group developing policy in this area. He has also worked with the UK government's academies programme in establishing two new secondary schools, and with the London Challenge as chair of a local School Improvement Partnership Board. In 2006 he became an accredited School Improvement Partner (SIP) within the New Relationship with Schools legislation, and worked in this capacity with schools in London and Essex.

In 2007 Clive became a freelance educational consultant, and has worked both nationally and internationally in this capacity. He has extensive experience and expertise in both leading and delivering school improvement initiatives within the areas of continuing professional development, the leadership of teaching and learning and targeted support for the able, gifted and talented. In 2008–9 he was living and working in China where he gained further insight into the learning needs of the exceptionally able.

How to use this book

Researching this book made it abundantly clear that there is now a wealth of material freely available on the internet to anyone seeking to improve or update their knowledge and understanding of able, gifted and talented education. So much so, that one way to use this book is to turn immediately to the final section and use the bibliographical material provided to compile a personal – indeed a personalised – library of bookmarked special interest sites, electronic articles, government-sponsored downloads and e-learning modules sufficient to acquire either a working knowledge of the entire field or else an authoritative take on a particular area of current professional concern.

As always, however, the problem for working teachers and other professionals is one of time. From this perspective alone the material gathered here seeks to offer a clear and relatively concise summary of an increasingly important area of educational provision for busy managers, project leaders, classroom practitioners and learning support staff. In a context in which significant emphasis is being placed on the need for schools to develop personalised pathways for all learners, there is still a clear need for an up-to-date overview of good practice and organisational opportunity in relation to able, gifted and talented (AG&T) learners.

While the book is therefore unashamedly written to provide accessible guidelines for readers requiring a short-cut through current educational debates and national developments for the AG&T, its main purpose is not so much didactic as developmental. To this end, each chapter contains a range of prompts for professional development activities intended to be used by:

- *Individual readers* as a way of embedding the advice provided into their own professional practice

- *AG&T coordinators, lead practitioners and professional development providers* as a readily available source of material to engage colleagues in discussion about provision for more able learners in their own schools

- *School leaders* as part of a structured programme of audit, self-review and organisational improvement focused on meeting the needs of all learners through raised challenge, differentiated learning and personalised provision.

In this sense, the way to use this book is as a compendium of generic exemplar material and stimuli for promoting organisational reflection on the individualised needs of target schools, curriculum areas and teachers. Although the examples and activities provided aim to be of direct relevance to particular teaching and support contexts (i.e. they may be freely adopted and adapted for use in the classroom), they are primarily models of provision which must themselves be personalised to meet specialised subject and age-specific requirements. In this they provide models of approaches to teaching and learning which require the active professional understanding of teachers to make them applicable to their own situations.

Chapter 1   considers the development of whole-school policy and the need to align policy development to the wider ethos of the school/setting and its identified (audited) areas for improvement.

Chapter 2   goes on to examine how AG&T learners are perceived and defined within the school and its teaching and learning policy. It offers a range of activities to support schools in arriving at a consensus agreement with regard to terminology and the categorisation of able learners.

Chapter 3   considers a wide range of identification procedures for AG&T youngsters. Again professional development activities are included to assist schools in arriving at identification mechanisms that match their own ethos and cohort profile.

Chapter 4   focuses on the whole-school aspects of provision, including learning environment, cross-curricular planning and organisational support for the development of personalised learning.

Chapter 5   explores aspects of classroom provision including the role of higher order thinking, differentiated planning, creative learning and personalisation. Models of suggested approaches are provided for individual guidance and to support professional development activity generally.

Chapter 6   extends the concept of personalisation into the extra-curricular support provided for the more able learner and his/her parents. A range of audit strategies are suggested and opportunities provided to establish a developmental agenda for this area of the school's work.

Appendix   a number of the planning models and activities used throughout this book draw on a generic version of *Goldilocks and the Three Bears* specifically adapted for this purpose. The version used is set out in the Appendix.

Throughout the chapters you will encounter the following icons:

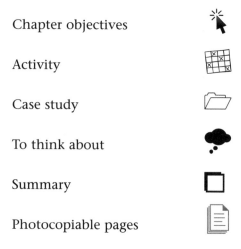

Chapter objectives

Activity

Case study

To think about

Summary

Photocopiable pages

NB: It should be noted that the acronym **AG&T** is used throughout to refer to the target group of learners. As Chapter 2 in particular will reveal, this is by no means an internationally accepted term and individual schools/settings may well decide on an alternative formulation better suited to local ethos and need. It goes without saying that what such youngsters are called is less important than the provision made to secure their entitlement as learners.

1

Developing school policy

> **Institutions developing effective policy for AG&T recognise that:**
> - Policy is the key to establishing and safeguarding effective practice
> - There is no 'one-size-fits-all' solution to policy development and discrete AG&T policies can either stand alone or be linked to more generic teaching and learning and/or inclusion policies
> - Policies need to be as unique as the institutions in which they are formulated.

All schools have a policy for their able learners, even if the policy is not to have a formal policy. Such an approach is not necessarily an indication of institutional inertia or complacency but can derive from the sincerely held educational philosophy that the most educationally advantaged youngsters will automatically gain most from the provision on offer and that diverting attention, effort and resources from the more needy is both unnecessary and, to the degree that it is socially unjust and elitist, potentially wrong.

The expectation that cream will automatically rise to the top, however, is not endorsed by experience. As with all learners, the more able, the highly able, those with marked aptitude(s) for particular area(s) of study, the gifted, the talented (to use only some of the more common designations for youngsters with high potential and/or attainment), vary significantly in their progress, self-awareness and overall performance in school.

Some of the reasons underlying the phenomenon of gifted underachievement will be examined in Chapters 2 and 3 of this book but the trend for able, gifted and talented (AG&T) youngsters generally to feature as an underperforming pupil group in our schools and colleges is well recognised. At the time of writing, for example, a controversy has arisen in England regarding the reported one in seven (11,500+) GCSE students on central government AG&T programmes nationally who failed in 2007 to achieve five subjects, including English and mathematics at grade C or above – a level of attainment generally associated not with high ability but with performance at expected levels.

To enshrine the view that young people of all abilities are entitled to equal consideration as learners, the 1988 Education Act in England decreed that an acceptable curriculum must be 'broad, balanced, relevant and *differentiated*' (emphasis added). This emphasis on individual entitlement prompted schools to consider the different learning needs of pupils across the whole ability range when drawing up policies to ensure the effective delivery of the curriculum. In common with many other countries, this drive to give pupils access to an education that matches individual requirements and guarantees continuity and progression in learning for all has since been at the heart of many schools' development of policy and practice in relation to their AG&T youngsters. In 2004, for English schools, the Children's Act and Every Child Matters legislation consolidated this principle by adding the concept of *personalisation* to that of differentiation as a guarantor of a child's right to an education that takes account of his or her strengths and weaknesses as a learner.

Can Quality Standards provide a starting point?

For English schools, National Quality Standards have been released which may have a wider currency elsewhere. These are broad benchmarks against which schools can audit and assess their current level of provision for AG&T. In essence these standards provide a range of performance indicators and descriptors against which to measure institutional development. The school policy standard outlines three levels of acceptable performance:

- *Entry level.* The gifted and talented policy is integral to the school/college's inclusion agenda and approach to personalised learning, feeds into and from the school/college improvement plan and is consistent with other policies.

- *Developing level.* The policy directs and reflects best practice in the school/college, is regularly reviewed and is clearly linked to other policy documentation.

- *Exemplary level.* The policy includes input from the whole-school/college community and is regularly refreshed in the light of innovative national and international practice.

For settings seeking more detailed progression lines for policy development the National Association for Able Children in Education (NACE) has a comprehensive Challenge Award package (see www.nace.co.uk for details).

What factors should be taken into account in developing policy?

Clearly, any whole-school policy needs to be informed by the school's own profile with regard to pupil ability and performance as well as by its wider approach to learning, teaching and school improvement. There is no 'one-size-fits-all' policy document that can be bolted on to a unique organisation to ensure that the specific needs of its more able cohort will be appropriately met. There are, however, a number of common considerations to be taken into account in developing a document that aligns the school's individual requirements to the overall objective of establishing an environment where high achievement is expected, planned for and celebrated. Any development of policy should:

- Be in line with the wider Teaching and Learning (T&L) Policy and/or any departmental or subject-specific curriculum policies (e.g. literacy or science) that seek to define and establish the organisational view of best practice in curriculum delivery and pupil engagement. It is even possible for the AG&T policy to be an integral part of the T&L and subject-specific policies and, for example, specify the particular approach to AG&T provision within individual curriculum areas

- Take account of the audit/analysis of pupil performance data and other assessment evidence revealing the impact of current provision on pupils' learning to identify and plan to address area(s) of relative weakness and/or underperformance in the overall profile of more able learners across the school (see Chapter 3)

- Be informed by the aims and objectives identified through the annual process of school self-evaluation and formalised in the appropriate whole-school improvement planning document

- Establish an agreed definition of able, gifted and talented pupils within the context of the school and its overarching educational ethos (Chapter 2)

- Provide clear identification strategies for the pupils who are to be the subject of modified and/or enhanced provision (Chapter 3)

- Support whole-school and classroom-based strategies for securing inclusion and appropriate levels of challenge for AG&T learners (Chapters 4 and 5)

- Explicitly establish that supporting AG&T pupils is the responsibility of all staff and not simply that of specific post-holders

- Specify any particular provision to be made for exceptionally able or talented individuals

- Clarify the nature of the provision to be made to support target groups, reflecting the development of a personalised, flexible and differentiated learning experience for all pupils

- Take account of the views of parents/carers and other stakeholders and partners, including evidence derived from pupils' own perceptions of learning in the school (Chapter 6)

- Include an action plan to map out and establish roles, responsibilities and monitoring/evaluation protocols with regard to the plan to ensure that it is driven through the organisation and updated as appropriate.

Audit or why is the policy needed?

What a policy needs to achieve is directly linked to the problems it has to address. This is why a starting point for policy creation is an audit to identify key issues relating to AG&T learners in the school. Data relating to pupil starting points or prior attainment at the start of school or key stage, to pupil progress or achievement over time and to attainment in national or school-based assessments will provide an important body of information about the size of the AG&T cohort, the nature of the progress made by individuals and groups both generally and in particular subject areas and about the impact of the current provision on the measured outcomes for target pupils. Clearly, the nature and extent of the available data will differ between settings but an audit will certainly reveal important information about the effectiveness of the school in supporting the achievement and attainment of its AG&T pupils relative to other pupil groups. Typical findings could include:

- A lower or higher number of pupils with above average scores either across the board or in particular areas on entry to the school

- Below average attainment at the higher levels at the end of Key Stage or public examination assessments when compared to that of schools in similar statistical contexts

- Relatively limited progress for pupils with high starting points, for example across a phase of education when compared to similar pupils in more effective schools and/or to other, more rapidly progressing pupil groups in the focus school

- Significant imbalances in attainment or progress at the highest levels among pupils of a particular gender or social or ethnic group contrary to national contextual value-added trends or to the performance of this/these group(s) in other curriculum areas within the school or in other statistically analogous schools

- A decline in attainment and/or progress patterns over time for pupils with the highest starting points suggesting that school improvement targets set for the most able on the basis of traditional value-added expectations are unlikely to be realised

- Evidence that individual youngsters on the school AG&T register or with the highest starting points/baseline assessment profiles make relatively less progress and/or attain less well in one particular curriculum area or age range than in others

- Evidence that particular public examination or assessment questions in a subject have been relatively poorly answered by otherwise able pupils in comparison to other questions in the test or to similar pupils in other schools.

It is impossible to be precise about the amount and quality of the performance data available to individual settings but for those schools within the jurisdiction of the UK Office for Standards in Education (Ofsted), the interactive Raiseonline software supports a wide range of school-level analyses relating to overall progress and attainment patterns, group monitoring, individual pupil tracking and performance analysis within a sophisticated contextual value-added formula providing schools with an accurate picture of their performance on a relative percentage scale across a wide range of indicators. Where Raiseonline is not available or appropriate, other performance data such as setting-specific baseline assessment information taken on entry to nursery, Early Years Foundation Stage Profile Assessments taken at rising 5, predictive IQ testing or summative end-of-year tests, should also be used as part of the wider audit process.

Case study

The following case studies, one primary, the other secondary, exemplify information drawn from audit. Consider the following questions:

1. What is the data telling the school about priorities for improving AG&T performance?

2. What additional information would it be useful to know before deciding on appropriate action?

Primary

At age 5 assessment consistently shows over 50% of children achieving in the top 20% of the assessment scale in all elements of communication, language and literacy. A smaller percentage (over 25%) consistently achieve at the highest point on the scale in the three elements of problem-solving, reasoning and numeracy. These outcomes show no clear gender, sub-group or ethnic bias.

End of infant phase assessments (age 7) at the highest level available – have been consistent for the past four years and this year at over 50% are more than twice the national average (n/av) in mathematics (48% of girls; 52% of boys).

In English 23% achieved highest level in reading. This was just on n/av for girls and slightly below for boys. In writing 25% achieved highest level, almost twice n/av with 28% of girls (n/av 17%) and 22% of boys (n/av 9%).

In terms of national attainment tables the school is:

• in the top 5% for mathematics at the highest level compared to similar schools

• in the lowest 40% for reading at the highest level with boys in the bottom 25%.

End of junior phase assessments (age 11) at the highest level available – were well above average in mathematics with 66% overall (40% girls; 83% boys).

In reading 70% overall achieved highest level (85% girls; 57% boys).

In writing, 52% were at the highest level (80% of girls (n/av 24%); 22% of boys (n/av 15%)).

In terms of national attainment tables for comparable schools the school is:

• in the top 10% for mathematics attainment (boys top percentile, girls top 50%) and in top 25% for progress with girls on the 50th percentile, boys top percentile

(Continued)

(Continued)

- in reading in the top 10% for attainment (girls top 5%; boys top 25%) and for progress in the top percentile overall and for boys and girls separately

- in writing in the top 5% overall for attainment (girls top percentile; boys top 40%) and for progress girls top percentile and boys on the 50th percentile.

Secondary (girls school)

Girls at the **highest level on entry at 11** = well below n/av over last five years. Mathematics 7% (n/av 33%); reading 15% (n/av 50%); writing 7% (n/av 19%); science 18% (n/av 45%).

School entry baseline testing = verbal reasoning 36% at 100+ with 11% at 120+. Non-verbal reasoning 31% at 100+ with 9% at 120+.

At age 14 figures show declining trend over last three years despite stable baseline figures on entry. In English highest level outcomes are 6% this year, down from high of 22%. This puts the school in the lowest 25% for similar schools nationally. In mathematics 39% reached the highest level which reflects a year-on-year increase and the school now features in the top 25% of similar schools. In science 13% reach the highest level (just above the lower quartile for similar schools). Progress is therefore unsatisfactory for those more able in English and above expected levels in mathematics.

Attainment age 16 shows 10% achieve five or more highest grades (including English and mathematics) and 37% achieving five or more passing grades. This is below n/av for attainment but shows above expected levels of progress for upper ability pupils from age 11 to 16 and from 14 to 16, where well above expected levels of progress were made in English.

Commentary

There are many things that could be said about each example but the following points should be considered:

1. The **primary school data** suggests that within the context of a highly advantaged intake there are clear issues about the progress of more able children in reading age 5–7 (particularly for boys), suggesting that this is an area where challenge, higher order reading skills and perhaps gender appropriateness within the curriculum could be improved. Gender continues to be an issue age 7–11 where girls do relatively better in reading and writing than boys while the reverse is true for mathematics.

2. The **secondary school data** shows a more disadvantaged intake generally with issues relating to attainment and progress of the more able in English age 11–14. This is reversed age 14–16 where challenge would seem to exist. Although comparatively few numerically, the school appears to be supporting the progression of its able pupils (approximately 1 in 10 on entry age 11).

3. Beyond the story told by the data it would be useful to know:

   - What assessment data reveals about achievement in foundation areas (e.g. humanities, art, etc.)

- What type(s) of learning experience produced positive and more negative outcomes for AG&T pupils/groups (including standardised assessment tasks that were well or poorly done)

- Information about provision for high achievement/talented behaviour currently existing in areas beyond the core curriculum

- Examples of excellence or individual AG&T behaviour which reveal the success or the limitations of current provision

- The views of staff, AG&T pupils and carers with regard to the current provision and how it might be improved.

What further information can be gathered through audit?

Data on pupil performance is clearly an important factor in determining the key issues for school policy to address. It will often (as with the primary case study) reveal that underperformance (or lack of satisfactory progress) as opposed to underattainment (not achieving high grades) is a significant factor among pupils of high potential. Audit, however, also requires more qualitative information if it is to provide a fuller picture of the needs of the school and the AG&T individuals within it. The following list itemises some of the ways in which a review of provision can lead towards a fuller understanding of an organisation's current practice and the developments necessary for AG&T policy to underwrite its practice:

- An examination of work produced by a sample of AG&T children from across the school (particularly where data has revealed areas of concern, areas of conspicuous success and areas in which data is unavailable or inconclusive). This will give a clearer understanding of the type of work/questioning, etc. which produces the most positive responses (see Chapter 4 for an appropriate framework of evaluation)

- A question-level analysis of standardised assessment tests (available to English schools through Raiseonline) revealing areas of relative weakness in AG&T response to questions

- A survey of departments, post-holders, teachers and staff to identify, collect and collate provision for AG&T currently operating either formally or informally

- Focus group discussions with AG&T pupils to ascertain their views on their academic and other provision: what they enjoy, what they find less successful and areas they would like to see improved better to meet their learning and developmental needs. A similar focus group with parents/carers could also be considered

- A programme of lesson observations (where time is short, concentrating on areas of relative weakness, success and curriculum areas from which little objective information is available)

- Pupil shadowing whereby a representative sample of AG&T children or one focus child are/is tracked/observed and interviewed as follow-up across a period of time – a day, a week, in a particular curriculum area, in individual lessons across a half-term, etc. – with the aim of drawing up an evidence-base and/or individual case-studies for professional examination on issues such as level of challenge, degree of engagement, etc. (see the suggested observation pro forma, Figure 1.1)

- Whole-staff discussion of the issue(s) of AG&T across the school (informed by evidence from preliminary audit findings) with a view to soliciting opinion, gathering evidence, reviewing/developing case studies and defining parameters.

How does the policy relate to the school's aims and values?

Whatever the audit reveals about the developmental needs of the school with regard to its AG&T pupils, there are usually several legitimate ways of addressing the emergent issues. Here are some common findings:

- The need to raise attainment generally, through increased challenge and opportunity

- The desire to attract a greater proportion of more able children to the school to secure a broadly mixed-ability intake

- The need to develop pupils as independent learners and so more actively develop their academic potential

- Concern over underachievement and/or low levels of value-added attainment at higher performance levels

- Concerns relating to a particular group of pupils whose potential is less likely to be translated to performance than others

- Concerns linked to low(er) attainment in a particular curriculum area

- The need to improve high-level provision to meet advanced needs in a particular target area (e.g. technology, sport, music)

- The need to ensure equality of opportunity within an inclusive curriculum for able pupils whose learning entitlements generally are not currently so explicitly met as those of other (groups of) children

- The desire to provide a greater variety of learning styles to meet the needs of learners whose aptitudes are not met by current provision

- The need to improve school performance figures and hit targets set by heads and governors, the local authority and central government.

Lesson Observation Pro Forma (Able, Gifted and Talented focus)

Class/year group	Lesson/subject	Period/time	Date	Male	Female
Teacher	**Focus of obervation** (e.g. pupil tracking, ILP, challenge, personalisation, etc.)				
Context of lesson (e.g. practical skills, group activity, independent research, etc.)					

Learning (Gains in skills, thinking, knowledge and understanding? Do pupils meet the lesson's learning objectives, make appropriate progress, understand what they have learned and know how to improve?)

Teaching (Comment on differentiation, personalisation, higher order thinking, open-endedness, advanced skills, appropriate challenge, high expectations, pace and variety, quality of questioning, assessment for learning)

Attitudes (Comment on levels of application, concentration, consistency, cooperation, collaboration, enthusiasm, self-awareness and motivation, etc.)

NB: Judgements of (1) good or better; (2) satisfactory; or (3) unsatisfactory may be made for each of the criteria.
Note the impact of any AG&T initiative observed in the classroom (e.g. mentoring).

Figure 1.1

While most of these objectives are not mutually exclusive, they do suggest contrasting approaches and values. Whatever else a school seeking to recruit more AG&T learners might do, it will certainly need to consider staging various high-profile events to attract the attention of parents and the local community. Some raising-achievement initiatives, however, may be better served by the steady promotion of curriculum change from within the school.

Some issues, however, can be addressed in a variety of ways, which will often depend on philosophical views of education and child development. For example, should a 7-year-old who is very able in mathematics be allowed to do her mathematics lessons with the class above or will her needs better be met through enrichment/extension work undertaken with her own peers? Clearly, the needs of children should come above any educational orthodoxy and one answer to this question resides in discovering exactly how exceptional this individual girl is. Equally certainly, however, the overriding values or ethos of the school will also be a consideration in this matter. Does the school freely support the principle of accelerated setting or is the view taken that children will generally be more emotionally secure among their peers in all bar the most compelling cases? It is issues such as this one that will need deciding upon and incorporating into the policy as part of a statement of key values before any decision is made on the exact nature of the provision to be developed.

For this reason, it is vital that policy making is explicit at first about the aims, values and philosophical rationale that underpin the provision that it is the job of the policy to outline and secure.

Activity

Read the following statements which might form the introduction to a whole-school policy on AG&T. Decide which is the closest fit to your own school's ethos with regard to this area of provision. You might wish to note down or underline parts of any statement that accord with your own thinking. Feel free to add any missing element of provision. This should allow you to come up with a model close to the one you would want to inform your policy.

NB: This activity can be productively undertaken during a professional development session.

1. At [School X] provision for more able pupils will be as inclusive as possible and seek to provide for the needs of this group of children (both identified and those as yet unidentified) through appropriate differentiation, and extension opportunities developed and delivered through the mainstream curriculum. It will be the responsibility of each subject area to provide appropriate challenge for high-attaining pupils within that area. In addition, a programme of enrichment opportunities based on lunchtime and after-school clubs will be made available to all children. Such activities will further broaden the provision made by the school to help children develop individual interests and personal skills.

2. At [School Y] pupils identified and placed on the Gifted and Talented register will be eligible for one hour's targeted support each week with a trained learning mentor. This will allow time for an individualised learning plan (ILP) to be drawn up to address identified needs. In conjunction with the class teacher(s) provision could include:

- Individualised work set by the class teacher in line with the ILP

- Withdrawal from target lessons to receive advanced tuition in a particular area alongside similarly targeted pupils

- Acceleration in an area(s) of particular strength by taking lessons with a higher year group and so securing a better match of content to learning need

- An invitation to attend the school's Gifted and Talented Saturday classes

- In exceptional circumstances the promotion of not more than one academic year.

3. At [School Z] in line with a personalised approach to learning, AG&T pupils will be encouraged and facilitated in developing flexible pathways to learning. A personalised approach to learning will be available in which an extended school day will allow for a wider range of study and recreational options; the use of ICT and subscription to virtual learning environments will facilitate a closer match of study to ability; learning partnerships with neighbouring schools and/or higher educational institutions will allow for greater breadth of opportunity and a significantly enhanced faculty of creativity and thinking will support students in developing their own ability to apply learning in a productive manner.

What does the school aim to provide for gifted and talented pupils?

Although the three ethos statements above can to some extent merge within a comprehensive whole-school provision it is clear that each represents a particular conception of how best to meet identified need. If the aim is to focus on an identified 5–10% pupils for targeted support, it is still legitimate to ensure that 100% of pupils have access to teaching strategies designed to promote higher level thinking. One legitimate response to the range of possible approaches is to say 'well it all depends on what you mean by gifted and talented'. Chapter 2 will discuss issues of definition and Chapter 3 those of identification. Chapter 4 will look in detail at the strengths and weaknesses of particular types of provision. At this stage, it is important to recognise that all children, not just the AG&T, will benefit from good practice in teaching and learning, from effective differentiation, from assessment for learning, including individual target setting; personalised learning and appropriate study support.

Accordingly, as schools consider their provision, the following generic strategies should be of relevance to the review:

- The processes of differentiation and personalisation, particularly in settings where the range of ability in classes is very wide

- Developing self-awareness among learners (learner identity), a range of learning styles to match all aptitudes, higher order thinking and independent learning skills as this all helps pupils make more effective use of the taught curriculum

- Linking self-awareness to developing procedures to foster 'student voice', whereby learners have the opportunity to express opinions on their learning and contribute to the school's self-evaluation processes

- Offering a broader curriculum beyond the statutory requirements, either through extra-curricular opportunities or an extended curriculum offer

- Providing some additional pastoral and/academic support (e.g. a learning mentor) particularly for pupils whose abilities make them exceptional within the context of their own peer group

- Incorporating enrichment and extension opportunities into schemes of work and programmes of study to routinely secure additional levels of challenge

- The role of setting and/or ability grouping within mixed classes

- Curriculum flexibility, where appropriate or possible, to allow learning pathways which genuinely meet individual need rather than administrative convenience (e.g. acceleration, promotion, short-term grouping for particular projects, partnership working, etc.)

- Assessment for learning giving pupils an ownership of their strengths and weaknesses and what they need to do to improve (using, as appropriate, individual target setting to secure improvement).

To think about

- What would be a realistic timetable in which to draw up an appropriate AG&T policy?

- Should the lack of a completed policy halt development of practice and provision for AG&T pupils or can the two go hand in hand within an action research context?

- Who will be involved in steering the development process – a single post-holder, a group of interested parties, the Senior Leadership Team, delegated area representatives?

- What role will there be for pupils and parents to contribute (pupil voice)?

- What professional development will be required to initiate, develop and sustain provision and how can this be built into the ongoing cycle of school improvement?

Summary

Some key points and suggestions have been made in this chapter in relation to developing school policy for AG&T learners.

- Policy making for AG&T is intrinsically linked to the drive to improve Teaching and Learning in the school.

- Drawing up policy is not about ticking boxes to ensure compliance with external expectations but about securing the entitlement of a significant group of learners to an effective education.

- Audit should precede policy formulation to target areas of need but audit needs to be both quantitative (based on performance data/indicators) and qualitative (drawing on stakeholder interviews, work scans, lesson observations and desk-top review of current curricular planning).

2

Defining able, gifted and talented

> **Arriving at a suitable definition requires clarity of purpose about:**
> - The contrasting range of overlapping terms and concepts available in discussing high ability
> - The organisational ethos underpinning the agreed definition
> - The availability of generic definitions and how they might be used to scaffold a whole-school formula
> - Theoretical models of gifted performance and how they relate to learners and learning within the school
> - Appropriate professional development activities to achieve consensus.

The purpose of this chapter is to prompt consideration of what the school policy means when it refers to able, gifted and talented children. This question is not merely one of abstract or academic definition. Being clear about the terms makes it easier to be clear about which youngsters the terms describe. This is why defining the cohort must precede the task of identifying the cohort discussed in Chapter 3. Moreover, the way high ability is understood has a significant impact on the way in which it is taught. In this sense there is a direct correspondence between the type(s) of provision established to meet AG&T needs in the school (see Chapter 4) and the school's defined view of how its most able pupils can best succeed as learners.

Activity

This may be attempted individually but is best done in pairs. It may be used as an introduction to the topic of definition within a professional development programme. It is a useful brainstorming exercise to help establish current thinking before reading the rest of the chapter.

The task is to note down (and agree) brief definitions for each of the following words/phrases:

(Continued)

(Continued)

- Giftedness
- Talent
- Exceptional performance
- Creativity
- Intellectual
- Intellectual capacity
- High ability
- High attainment
- High achievement
- High flyer
- Exceptionally gifted
- Great potential

- Exceptional ability
- Intelligence
- Above-average ability
- Skill
- Aptitude
- Marked-aptitude
- Outstanding
- Excellent
- Prodigy
- Academic
- Genius

If used as part of a professional development programme (PDP), the following method may be employed.

Make the words available and ask pairs/small groups to sort the list into synonyms and words with a singular meaning. Then arrive at a common definition for any perceived synonym groups and distinctive definitions for words with distinctive implications (NB: 'Post-it' notes stuck to flip chart paper are an effective and visually striking way of organising this). Take feedback regarding the list of different terms and concepts so identified. Try to arrive at some agreed overview and go on to discuss the range of different categorisations within the topic. Work towards answering the question 'what do the differences imply about learners so described'? (Timing ranges from 20 minutes for an individual activity to 45 minutes as a PDP activity.)

The point of this activity is threefold:

1. It suggests the very large number of potentially vague terms that educationalists use to describe high ability and so reveals some of the problems of terminology and definition faced by policy-makers in this area.

2. It indicates how the language used to describe and define an able child within the school relates to the school's ethos with regard to ability and what particular aspects of the AG&T agenda it seeks to support.

3. It provides an opportunity via feedback and discussion to arrive at some initial school-based consensus within the somewhat shifting sands of definitions and educational perspectives surrounding AG&T performance.

Some given definitions

Happily for schools looking to develop their own definitions of AG&T, there are a number of high profile formulations available internationally which are intended for adoption/adaptation by individual organisations. The most influential of these is **The Marland Definition** produced in 1972 by the then US Commissioner of Education for use in state and local education agencies. It states that:

> Gifted and talented children are those identified by professionally qualified persons who, by virtue of outstanding abilities, are capable of high performance. These are children who require differential educational programs and/or services beyond those provided by the regular school program in order to realize their contribution to self and the society.
>
> Children capable of high performance include those with demonstrated achievement and/or potential ability in any of the following areas, singly or in combination –
>
> • General intellectual ability;
>
> • Specific academic aptitude;
>
> • Creative or productive thinking;
>
> • Leadership ability;
>
> • Visual and performing arts;
>
> • Psychomotor ability.
>
> (Marland, 1972)

The carefully crafted Marland formulation has been used extensively to inform policy in America and around the world. It has also met with widespread (though not universal) academic approval. Eighty per cent of experts and organisations polled before its release agreed that high intellectual ability, creative or productive thinking, specific academic aptitude, and ability in visual or performing arts should be key elements of any overarching definition. However, only half agreed that leadership and psychomotor ability should be included. In England the Schools' Council issued a remarkably similar definition in which physical talent, artistic talent, mechanical ingenuity, leadership, high intelligence and creativity were the six criteria for high attainment, taking in an estimated 30–40% of any given cohort.

Clearly, academic and professional reassessments over four decades will bring new emphases to almost any educational formula. This is particularly the case where social change redefines attitudes and modifies traditional values. The current US federal prescription, for example, reflects the cultural shift towards science and information technology by defining (for funding purposes) a gifted student more narrowly as one who 'demonstrates actual or potential high performance capability in the fields of mathematics, science, foreign languages, or computer learning' (US Regulations for the Educational Security Act, 1984, cited by Mary Codd at www.riage./org/gifteddef.html).

It is always the case that definitions of excellence encapsulate the social values and aspirations of their time and place. No modern definition, for example, would prioritize rhetoric as an essential accomplishment of a gifted individual and yet for the ancient Greeks and Romans it was exactly that. In China today, the traditional Confucian cultural view that giftedness is not an innate ability but the outcome of *talented performance developed through effort* colours the official determination to extend gifted provision not to the estimated 3 million or so youngsters with IQ scores of 130 plus but to the 200 million estimated to be of above-median intelligence so that many more children can work hard to develop their talents in all areas for the benefit of an emerging superpower and its growing economy.

Similarly in England, the recent definition provided by central government through the Young, Gifted and Talented programme to promote the development of personalised provision for the able is underwritten by the socially inclusive ethos of The Children's Act. Its aim is to address underachievement and support the most disadvantaged, in attainment, aspirations, motivation and self-esteem. Accordingly, the definition offered to the profession by the Department for Children, Schools and Families is broadly based, egalitarian and school-focused:

> Gifted and talented learners are defined as those who have one or more abilities developed to a level significantly ahead of their year group (or with the potential to develop those abilities).
>
> Gifted describes learners who have the ability to excel academically in one or more subjects such as English, drama, technology.
>
> Talented describes learners who have the ability to excel in practical skills such as sport, leadership, artistic performance, or in an applied skill.
>
> Our policy starts from the expectation that there are gifted and talented learners in every year group in every school. It is up to each school to decide on the proportion of their population who are gifted and talented. Since we believe that ability is evenly distributed throughout the population, a school's gifted and talented pupils should be broadly representative of its whole school population. (www.standards.dfes.gov.uk/giftedandtalented/who/)

Why not simply adopt an available definition?

The definitions set out in the previous section can help to scaffold an individual school's strategy towards AG&T. Each definition, however, reveals differences of emphasis and ethos to be considered before wholesale adoption. Questions to be asked include:

- Which aspects of the model definition(s) specifically address the needs of the organisation as revealed through audit (Chapter 1)?

- Does the ethos of the model in whole or in part accord with that of the school and the nature of the provision it seeks to develop?

- Is the funding available likely to be sufficient to underwrite broadly inclusive policy and provision or do local resourcing priorities dictate a more targeted approach to defining AG&T within the school?

- Do 'off-the-shelf' definitions of gifted and talented behaviour need to be evaluated and possibly combined before arriving at a definition that best fits the developmental agenda of the school improvement plan?

Cross-reference

The following summaries of earlier and current theories relating to the AG&T performance should be compared and contrasted with the national definitions already examined. Consider any features of the research that seem valuable within your school context but which do not feature strongly in any or all of the given models.

IQ and the measurement of general intellectual ability

In the early twentieth century Alfred Binet developed an IQ test to predict those who would do well in school and those who would need additional support. This work was extended by Lewis Terman who developed the idea of intelligence quotient as almost the sole arbiter of giftedness. He went on to suggest a classification scheme which is still in use today and in which a score of 135 is described as 'moderately gifted', above 150 as 'exceptionally gifted' and above 180 as 'severely and/or profoundly gifted'. It will be necessary to return to IQ as an identifier of giftedness in Chapter 3, but, in the context of definition and the measurement of general intellectual ability, questions for schools include:

- At what cut-off point should an abstract reasoning test or tests indicate that a pupil becomes eligible for consideration as one of the AG&T cohort?

- Should the definition distinguish between pupils scoring – say – 120+ (able), 135+ (gifted) and 150+ (exceptionally gifted), given that the provision made for an individual at 150 will need to be as different from that of someone at 120 as the provision for a 120 will need to be from that of those scoring 90?

- Ought the formula reflect absolute IQ scores or should provision be relative to the school cohort, so that a grammar school would routinely expect to meet the needs of its numerous 120 IQ band pupils through normal practice, making targeted support unnecessary, whereas a school with high incidence of disadvantage may need to consider differentiated provision for any student with a score above 115?

- How should primary schools address the issue of measuring intelligence when standardised tests are unavailable and/or considered inappropriate as a measurement of potential ability?

- Is it possible and/or desirable to augment or substitute abstract reasoning tests with more subjective gauges of potential intellectual ability such as language development, conceptual awareness, memory and reasoning capability?

- Should a curriculum-specific solution be adopted to assess intellect based more on current attainment than measured potential, such as that recommended by the English Qualifications and Curriculum Authority in defining AG&T pupils as those that well exceed the expectations for their age-group, either in all subjects or just one (www.qcda.gov.uk/1957.aspx)?

Multiple intelligence

In one respect the notion of multiple intelligence, so far as defining AG&T is concerned, does little more than expand on the Marland suggestion that high ability can manifest itself as an aptitude for just one subject or academic area. There is, however, an important distinction. While multiple intelligence theory, as originally expounded by Howard Gardner, can explain why some pupils excel at art and others at music, it also suggests that individuals – by dint of their defining intelligence(s) – have one or more preferred learning style(s):

- Linguistic (using language in all its forms)

- Musical (including compositional, instrumental and vocal skills)

- Logical-mathematical (number, pattern, shape and deductive reasoning)

- Visual-spatial (seeing and manipulating objects physically and in abstract)

- Bodily-kinaesthetic (use of the whole body as in sport, dance and drama)

- Naturalist (using and being inspired by the natural world, natural sciences, etc.)

- Interpersonal (the sense of others and the social skills reliant on that sense)

- Intrapersonal (the sense of self and the ability to reflect on and evaluate the self).

The implication is that everyone brings their dominant style(s) to all areas of learning. The linguistic/intrapersonal learner, for example, will benefit from and enjoy lessons in which he/she is focused on language and allowed to consider its impact and meaning individually. A visual-spatial/interpersonal learner, however, will benefit much more from lessons involving diagrams, images and artefacts discussed in a group or collaborative context.

This insight clearly extends the recognition that there are particular types of gift-edness linked to particular types of achievement (academic, creative, social, etc.) towards the view that there are also particular types of learners. Here the question is not how bright the pupil is but how is the pupil bright? Embracing such a notion as part of the definition of high ability within the school not only raises issues concerning the range of learning styles supported by teaching across the whole curriculum but also the extent to which the provision encourages pupils to become aware of their own strengths and weaknesses as learners. In this context learning styles link powerfully to the development of personalised learning. The way in which a school identifies and communicates information about learning styles to the learner (assessment for learning), and the way in which learners themselves make use of their self-knowledge to maximise their opportunities are both key issues of provision (Chapter 4) which could be supported through the definitions of able learners written into the policy.

Ability, commitment and creativity

The Marland definition cites creativity as one facet of AG&T performance. For some this itemisation of creativity as one of six possible defining factors does not go far enough in highlighting the central role played by creativity in almost all socially purposeful educational outcomes. Multiple intelligence theory, for example, sees each intelligence as defining a particular type of problem-solving approach and creative capability.

The psychologist Joseph Renzulli divided giftedness into two main categories. The first (or *schoolhouse giftedness*) is associated with success in tests and quantifiable assessments. Such pupils are easy to identify though sometimes the potential revealed in IQ tests fails to translate into academic performance. The second category (*creative-productive giftedness*) relates to activity that puts high value on the development of original material or products designed to suit defined audiences. This is a key factor in ensuring productive outcomes emerge from the challenges of education and of life.

Paradoxically, some of the most gifted individuals in terms of measured potential fail to live up to that potential either in school or in life beyond formal education. One reason for the phenomenon of gifted underachievement is the tendency for some individuals to lack task commitment or the ability and/or desire to apply themselves to the challenges they are set or face. For some youngsters, the ease with which they meet the major challenges of their formative years (e.g. language development, concept development, literacy, numeracy, abstract thought, etc.) means that they fail to develop the capacity, the psychological muscle, the work ethic that predisposes a person to try hard and meet the challenges of learning and life.

In this model of AG&T accomplishment there are three interdependent factors associated with achieving optimum performance – see Figure 2.1.

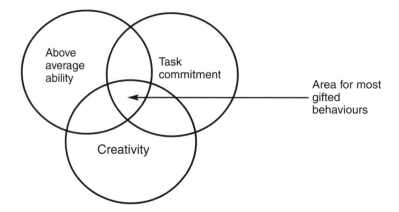

Figure 2.1 Renzulli's tripartite model of giftedness
Renzulli, J.S. (1994) 'New directions for the schoolwide enrichment model', *Gifted Education International*, 10(1): 33–6

Schoolhouse ability without creativity suggests a sterile mindset in which knowledge or accomplishment or skill has few productive outcomes for the individual or society. Creativity without task commitment is unlikely to produce sustained satisfactory outcomes. Optimum performance arises when talent tries hard to produce effective solutions.

Any definition of AG&T that seeks to incorporate this tripartite model of giftedness has to accept that provision needs to be made to develop creative working and task commitment alongside enhanced academic opportunities. The Chinese Confucian approach, for example, draws strongly on the social and cultural expectation of hard work. Often, however, it places far less emphasis on creativity and independent learning skills.

The challenge is to foster all three, working in unison. The opportunity is to improve creative working and staying power. Unlike measured intelligence (which unfortunately appears to be a given; a fixed determinant), creative capacity and power of application are more akin to muscles that can be developed through appropriate activity. Chapter 4 endeavours to address this challenge.

Defining giftedness from a child-centred perspective

Gifted children may often develop cognitively at a much faster rate than they do physically, socially and emotionally. This so-called *asynchronous development* can cause a number of problems for the gifted child, including:

- A mismatch between ideas or intentions and the physical inability to realise them

- Reading, thinking about or understanding issues and material they are not emotionally ready to handle

- Intellectual isolation from peers including difficulties in play resulting from more advanced interests

- A preference for older, even adult, company, which can be unwelcome or inappropriate.

Generally, the brighter the child the greater the mismatch between physical and mental development, and with this comes the greater potential for confusion, alienation, unhappiness and vulnerability.

Where such issues are perceived to cause problems for individuals, the resulting definition of AG&T children should allow for pastoral support and/or counselling to address the issue of susceptible youngsters.

Defining gifts and talents

The English central government formula defines giftedness in terms of the potential of a learner in one or more academic areas. Talent is defined in terms of excellence in an applied skill such as art or sport or leadership. This distinction between gifts and talents, however, is neither obligatory nor inevitable. The Chinese conception, for example, sees all potential as something to be developed through education and application into specific manifestations of talented performance. Within this model there is no philosophical or qualitative distinction drawn between high achievement in physics and high achievement in dance.

Making this point may appear to be little more than terminological quibbling with little practical relevance to the overall aim of maximising potential in schools. Alternatively, it may better match the inclusive ethos of some schools to describe all youngsters as similarly striving to realise their latent abilities. Whether these abilities are termed gifts, talents or even aptitudes is less important than their being described and valued equally.

This is an approach supported by Françoys Gagné (2004) whose model of giftedness and talent envisages gifts as natural abilities which grow – or don't grow – into talents not only through application but in association with all of the other influences and variables which impact on human performance – see Figure 2.2.

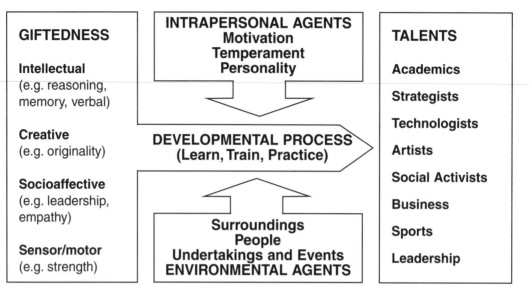

Figure 2.2 Gifts into talents model
Adapted from Gagné, F. (2004) 'Transforming gifts into talents: the DMGT as a developmental theory', *High Ability Studies*, 15(2): 119–47. Reprinted by kind permission of the publisher (Taylor & Francis Group, www.informaworld.com)

Here the natural abilities (gifts) reveal themselves as a facility for particular types of activity – the greater the gift the greater the ease of acquisition. The sensor/motor gift of dexterity, for example, will mean that its possessor will be naturally adept at any activity that requires this attribute, be it juggling or gymnastics. Talents, however, begin to emerge via the transformation of gifts through learning, training and practice into well-honed and systematically developed skills relating to a particular field of human activity or performance. Thus reasoning ability as a gift can be shaped into the skills required by a forensic scientist, a chess player or a computer programmer, but any such shaping ultimately depends on affirmative personal and environmental factors.

Key points for this model are:

- Gifts that are not developed remain as raw materials and represent under-achievement.

- The highest levels of talent require the most intensive development.

- The quality of the developmental process from gift to talent is shaped by school programmes and other formal agents and environmental influences which establish the 'nature of the nurture', but also by a more fluid and unpredictable variety of motivational characteristics, inherited predispositions or traits and acquired attitudes towards learning.

- Personal qualities such as determination, courage, cooperativeness and enthusiasm are as important as latent ability in securing the transition from potential to talented performance.

For potential to be deemed gifted and performance to be deemed talented it must by definition be above average. Significant deviation above the average in any normal distribution is considered by statisticians to begin beyond the 85th percentile and it is the top 15% of youngsters who are routinely targeted within this developmental context.

The size of target groups will, of course, vary from setting to setting for a diversity of reasons. One constant, however, is the understanding that high achievement requires positive attitudes. For schools to foster the individual curiosity, motivation, strength of purpose and simple joy in learning necessary to facilitate the journey towards talented performance may well be the most powerful way in which any intervention programme can support gifted young people. In this context, developing such personal qualities becomes a major objective of personalisation. Any definition drawing on recent research and socio-political expectations would do well to reflect this insight.

Activity

The following activities should help individuals, dedicated working parties or whole-staff groups work towards an agreed definition for AG&T in the school or setting.

Activity 1

Begin with the given definition that is closest to the formulation desired by the school or setting. From there, review the other theories discussed above and highlight any additional points which need to be added or taken into account in the final definition. On this basis produce a draft statement a to be reviewed and commented on by key stakeholders before finalising the formula.

Activity 2

In pairs agree on and label a picture of a composite AG&T pupil at the school or setting drawing on ideas taken from this chapter, school audit and improvement plans. Join each pair into a four to work collaboratively on an agreed picture and illustrative labels, captions, headings, etc. Finally snowball the fours into eight. Here each four presents its diagram to the other and the ultimate task is to construct a concept map incorporating all of the key terms and features to be included in the definition (see Figure 2.3).

Activity 3

From the introductory activity and the chapter as a whole decide which terms and descriptions will be used in your definition. Make sure you are clear about the implications of each term and how it relates to others you will use. Endeavour to structure your definition around these key terms and concepts (see Figure 2.4).

(Continued)

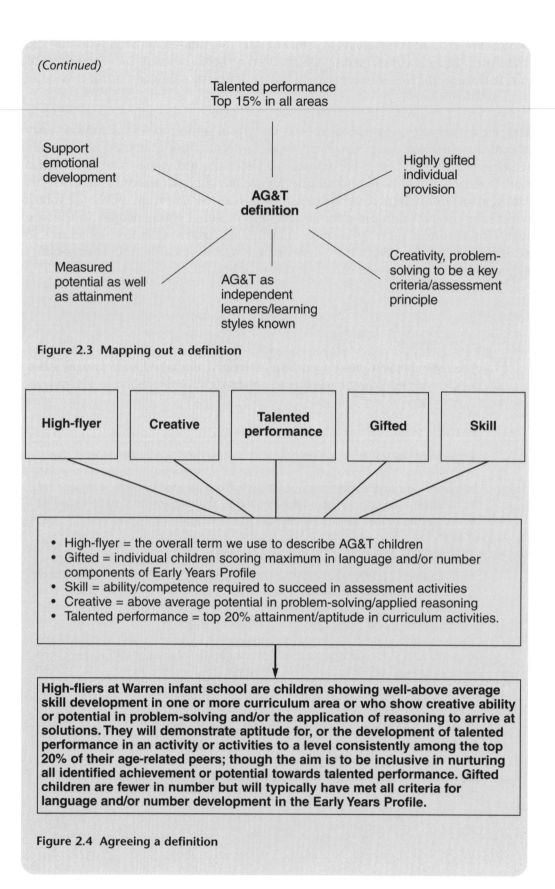

Figure 2.3 Mapping out a definition

Figure 2.4 Agreeing a definition

Summary

Some key points have been made in this chapter in relation to defining able, gifted and talented children.

- There are a variety of terms, definitions and theories linked to AG&T that are not always interchangeable.

- A school or setting should be clear about what it wants to achieve through its policy and not be tempted to 'bolt-on' definitions that do not support its ethos and improvement objectives.

- Involving all staff in professional development on the topic of AG&T will promote wider ownership of the policy.

3

Identifying the able, gifted and talented

> **Schools developing identifying procedures should consider:**
>
> - The relative weight to be given to quantitative measurements of ability against more qualitative professional judgements relating to performance and potential
> - How to combine multiple criteria and sources of evidence into a coherent whole-school procedure that fits the context of the school and the needs of its learning community
> - The nature of any professional development programme designed to provide staff with the necessary understanding and consensus of purpose to identify AG&T pupils effectively.

In England the current expectation is that all 11–19 settings should identify individuals meeting one or more of the national criteria for the top 5% of gifted and talented learners. The criteria include:

- A combined score in the national assessment tests (SATS) at age 11 in English and mathematics that is in the top 5% nationally

- A SAT level 8 or above in assessments taken at 14

- A merit or distinction pass in the UK World Class Tests for mathematics and problem-solving (age 8–11 or 12–14)

- Scores of 129 or above in any recognised standardised test for cognitive ability and reasoning (or above the 95th percentile on an IQ test)

- A score of 58 or above on examinations taken at 16 (i.e. 8 GCSEs at A/A*).

In addition, non-qualifying learners can be included among the top 5% through teacher nomination (and criterion-based reference); evidence of outstanding achievement outside of school (e.g. in debating, music or dance) or through the independent assessment of an educational psychologist.

The policy statement also recommends that schools and settings for ages 4–19 identify all learners deemed to be AG&T relative to their year group peers. While a widely based whole-school identification process will almost certainly reveal more youngsters than the narrowly defined top 5% of learners envisaged as being put forward for the national registration programme, it will reveal the target audience for the school's potentially more inclusive provision for its entire AG&T cohort. As we saw, this endeavour, taking into account undeveloped potential and a wider definition of talent, could incorporate more than one-third of any given cohort – more in areas of above-average social advantage.

The heavy emphasis on summative assessment for identifying the top 5% still allows room for professional judgement to figure in the selection criteria. It is clear that a school-based register with larger numbers, more flexible inclusion criteria and a wider conception of talented performance will draw even more extensively on informed teacher judgement as a key factor in the identification process. This is as it should be, because research (e.g. Denton and Postlethwaite, 1985) has consistently shown that *informed* teacher judgement is the most accurate means of identifying the range and diversity of AG&T learners across the school. For anyone leading on whole-school improvement in this area, however, it is important to note that the word 'informed' carries weight. Where staff are familiarised with the issues of identifying AG&T learners, a school is equipped to implement policy and improve practice. Without appropriate updating, however, it is likely that youngsters with more complex or latent areas of talent will be no more accurately identified than previously.

Any realistic criteria mapping the development of a school from satisfactory to exemplary practice implicity underwrites the need for staff training to support and sustain the required organisational improvement. The English Institutional Quality Standards (IQS), for example, sees satisfactory performance as having 'systems to identify gifted and talented pupils in all year groups' so as to keep 'an accurate record of the identified gifted and talented population'. Exemplary practice, however, emerges when 'multiple criteria and sources of evidence are used to identify gifts and talents' within 'a comprehensive monitoring, progress planning and shared reporting system to which all staff regularly contribute' (http://ygt.dcsf.gov.uk/FileLinks/930_qs.doc).

In Wales the NACE Challenge Award acts as the preferred model for informing school development, and here too schools are encouraged to draw on a wide range of assessment strategies to ensure that all types of abilities are recognised (see Department for Children, Education, Lifelong Learning and Skills, 2008: 24). In Scotland an analogous emphasis is placed on 'evidence from a broad range of sources, over time and across a range of activities, both in and out of school' (www.ltscotland.org.uk/curriculumforexcellence/assessmentandachievement/acrosslearning/index.asp).

The aim of this chapter therefore is to establish the range of factors which might inform professional judgement when identifying AG&T pupils. Within this, there are three overarching questions for consideration:

- What method(s) of identification may be used?

- What are the characteristics of AG&T pupils?

- How can we identify the learning needs of those pupils?

What methods of identification should be considered?

Any effective identification procedure needs to be an ongoing one. Best practice requires a continuous interplay between the challenges set by teachers, their monitoring of pupil responses to the work set and their identification of further challenges that meet each individuals' learning needs as revealed through these assessments. This ongoing loop connecting topic development, the assessment of learning needs and the further development and provision of appropriate challenge is the key to ensuring effective continuity and progression in learning for all youngsters. Ultimately, therefore, the quality of provision for AG&T learners depends on the quality of teacher observation and analysis. In this sense, 'bolt-on' identification procedures such as checklists and tests are of less value than rigorous assessment for learning practice in support of personalised approaches.

It should be remembered, however, that, for AG&T youngsters in particular, the nature of the work set needs to be of a type to readily elicit the sort of responses which will allow systematic insight into the higher order capabilities/advanced learning potential of the individual in question. In addition, because the indicators of AG&T responses to intellectual challenge are not always what might be intuitively expected, teachers – even those skilled in assessment for learning practice – need to be aware of the sometimes paradoxical indices of high ability. In these contexts, checklists and other criterion-referenced identification procedures are more useful in terms of broadening teacher awareness and/or encapsulating typical response patterns than they are as stand-alone identification tools.

Schools also need to consider which methods of identification sit comfortably alongside any earlier decisions made about the aims and ethos of the policy and their preferred definition(s) of AG&T. Other issues to bear in mind include:

- Identification should be a continuous, whole-school process informed by individual subject areas/departments and pastoral information

- The need to maintain rigour but also transparency, fairness and equality of opportunity

- Devising strategies for combining quantitative (test) data with qualitative information drawn from teacher assessment and observation

- Agreeing on the multiple sources of evidence to be used

- Ensuring that underachievers as well as high achievers are identified

- The desired 'mix' of pupils identified, including those with:

  i   potential as well as proven achievement

  ii   all-round ability and subject-specific strength

  iii   academic ability and creative ability.

- The desired involvement of pupils, parents and external agencies

- The practicality of the envisaged provision in terms of management, monitoring and updating

- The relationship between the AG&T register and the school community.

 Activity

This exercise introduces the range of identification procedures to the staff and provides an opportunity to consider each within the context of the school. For this to work as a group activity, at least eight participants (four groups of two) are needed. It can also work as an individual exercise to gain an overview of the options available.

Begin in pairs and provide each pair with one column from A, B, C or D from Figure 3.1. Where time is available give examples of each item for evaluation. The aim is for each pair to identify the pros and cons of using each identification strategy on their list. This should take 15–20 minutes. The next stage depends on numbers but requires the bringing together of one 'expert' from each pair into groups of four to produce mixed groups with at least one representative from each column (with larger staffs these mixed or 'rainbow' groups can be as large as eight). At this stage each expert – or expert pair – introduces their thinking on their four possible strategies. The aim of the mixed group is then to decide on the most appropriate of the 16 approaches for use in their particular school or setting (allow 30–40 minutes).

The objective is to provide a framework for discussing the pragmatic, educational and philosophical background to any identification strategy drawing on multiple criteria and sources of evidence. While schools must ensure that their chosen methodology and/or professional instruments for identifying AG&T conforms with their ethos, current working practices and (importantly) their current capacity, care should also be taken to ensure that an appropriate range of identification procedures (i.e. a range sufficient to meet the needs of all pupils) are finally agreed. Working through group feedback towards consensus can also help establish policy development and promote staff ownership. Figure 3.2 suggests some non-school-specific considerations for each approach.

Group A	Group B	Group C	Group D
National Curriculum Tests (National Tests at ages 7, 11, 14 and optional tests at 8, 9, 10, 12 & 13)	World Class Tests (mathematics and problem-solving for ages 9–13) www.worldclassarena.org	Subject-specific Checklists (criteria for high achievement in a specific area)	Classroom Observation and Pupil Profiling (plus Foundation Stage Profile)
National Curriculum Teacher Assessment	Ability Profile Tests (e.g. Wechsler Intelligence Scale for Children or Raven's Progressive Matrices)	Generic Checklists (general criteria for high or potential high achievers)	Parental Nomination
Assessment for Learning & Personalisation	Educational Psychologists (e.g. individual evaluation, IQ testing)	Creativity Tests (e.g. Torrance Tests of Creative Thinking and Urban & Jellen Test for Creative Thinking)	Work Scanning
Teacher Nomination	Progress Charts (e.g. Pupil Achievement Tracker)	Skill Tests (e.g. memory, reading, stamina, lateral thinking, etc.)	Self Assessment and/or Peer Assessment

Figure 3.1

METHOD	STRENGTHS	LIMITATIONS
National Curriculum Tests	• Curriculum based • Track progress over time • Link to national standards	• Underachievers not shown • Limited range of subjects • Only age 7–14
National Curriculum Teacher Assessment	• Clear QCA criteria • Full subject range • National Strategy Frameworks linked to learning objectives	• Underachievers not shown • Creativity • Possible subjectivity
Assessment for Learning and Personalisation	• Pupils identified through learning competencies as well as attainment • Learners aware of how to improve to meet learning targets/test criterion • Identification active and ongoing, not a fixed label	• Requires high quality formative assessment practice and staff training • An ongoing learning process works against a clearly identified/targeted AG&T cohort
Teacher Nomination	• Draws on teachers' ongoing assessments • Closely linked to classroom provision • Allows for extra-curricular achievement	• Subjective if not made against agreed criteria • Teaching may not reveal higher order/creative skills • Needs all teachers to participate or not equitable
World Class Tests for AG&T Pupils	• Modern ICT-based • Internationally standardised • Problem-solving element may help identify creative thinkers and/or unrealised potential • Several testing opportunities in each year	• Subject-specific element limited to mathematics • Linked to 9–13 age-range • Aimed at top 10% of ability so some prior identification is necessary • Potentially costly
Ability Profile Tests	• Useful for screening cohort • Objective measure of potential/latent ability • Standardised in comparison with others of similar age • Appropriate age 6–16	• Only measure limited range of competence (reasoning) • Do not reward divergent thinking or creativity • May be culturally or linguistically inaccessible to some pupils • Less robust towards the top of the scale (130+)

Figure 3.2 *(Continued)*

(Continued)

METHOD	STRENGTHS	LIMITATIONS
Educational Psychologist	• Invaluable in identifying high ability linked to complex issues, e.g. areas of SEN (dual exceptionality), behaviour difficulties, exceptional giftedness	• Time consuming and expensive. Unnecessary for most gifted pupils • Useful for specific individual diagnosis not for whole-cohort identification
Progress Charts	• Identify groups and individuals making exceptional progress over time • Reveal individual variations in performance across subject areas, phases, etc.	• Do not identify habitual gifted underachiever • Data emerges at end of phase (e.g. age 11 and 14) and so not effective for immediate identification or ongoing monitoring
Subject-specific Checklists	• Useful in assisting teachers to explore ability in subject-specific terms. • Discussion generated can inform teacher identification ability and improve task-setting	• Checklists cannot be relevant for each individual • Extensive lists can be complex and contradictory • Less useful with latent ability and with younger learners
Generic Checklists	• Easily accessible • Help broaden awareness	• May create stereotypes • Often difficult to relate to learning and curriculum • Can overlook non-generic youngsters
Creativity Tests	• Measures abilities not normally assessed as part of school assessment • Offers divergent thinkers a chance to display their ability	• Time consuming to administer • Subjective • Validity remains questionable
Skill Tests	• Can draw on known features of AG&T performance such as early or advanced reading, memory, three-dimensional thinking, hand–eye coordination, etc. • Simple to administer	• Will give indications rather than full screening • Suggest latent ability or potential rather than evolved performance
Classroom Observation and Pupil Profiling	• May broaden identification criteria • Assesses child in familiar context doing familiar tasks • Allows for school-based or age-specific criteria • Reveals variations in performance over time and between lessons or tasks	• Time consuming and therefore expensive • Implications for teacher workload • Can be subjective if not standardised • Needs to be ongoing to identify improvement, change, progress, etc.
Parental Nomination	• Intimate knowledge of the individual • Can take account of performance outside school environment	• Subjective and/or partial • Not professionally based • Needs to be used alongside other methods
Work Scanning	• Can be assessed against known criteria for AG&T • Tasks may be set to elicit AG&T response for identification purposes • Allows identification of individual variation within a subject or topic	• Can be subjective if not undertaken rigorously • Only measures achievement not potential • High performance reliant on opportunities to reveal talent (e.g. quality of questioning)
Self and/or Peer Assessment	• Allows pupil voice • Improves learner ownership of AG&T criteria and understanding of high achievement • Introduces learner perspective on learning	• Needs to be part of a wider identification process • Requires pupil induction to see high ability more broadly • Less robust with younger children

Figure 3.2 (Continued)

What are the characteristics of AG&T pupils?

There are many checklists available which list the characteristics of gifted children. An internet search for AG&T checklists will bring up many variations on the same theme. All have common strengths and weaknesses. General checklists are useful for revealing the range of behaviours and attitudes that *may* be exhibited by some AG&T learners, but equally plausibly may not. In this sense checklists are more useful as prompts for professional consideration than as the sole criteria for a whole-school identification process. *Identifying Gifted and Talented Learners – Getting Started* (2008: 3–5) published by the UK's Department for Children, Schools and Families cites checklists as one of eight approaches to draw on in formulating any whole-school identification procedure (alongside teacher nomination, testing, ongoing assessment, peer/parental nomination, discussion and the use of community resources).

Activity

Step One: The following checklists each itemise the characteristics of AG&T pupils from different perspectives. The task (which may be done singly, in pairs or as a larger development group), is to examine each list and identify/agree one main positive and one negative feature of the approach *from the point of view of your school/setting*. The aim is to decide which approach (or combined features of several approaches) will be most helpful in a checklist supporting the identification, nomination, screening, monitoring and mentoring of AG&T pupils (30 minutes).

1. Educational Psychologist approach

- Displays superior powers of reasoning, of dealing with abstractions, of generalising from specific facts, of understanding meanings and of seeing into relationships
- Shows great intellectual curiosity
- Learns easily and readily*
- Has a wide range of interests
- Reveals a broad attention span for problems and interests
- Demonstrates vocabulary and language skills significantly beyond those of peers
- Can work independently
- Learned to read early (sometimes before school age)*
- Has keen powers of observation
- Shows initiative and originality in intellectual work
- Is alert and responsive to new ideas
- Can memorise quickly

(Continued)

(Continued)

- Has great interest in the nature of man, the universe, origin and destiny at a young age

- Possess unusual imagination

- Follows complex directions easily

- Is a rapid reader*

- Has several hobbies

- Has reading interests which cover a wide range of subjects*

- Makes frequent and effective use of the library/information centre*

- Is superior in mathematics, particularly in problem-solving*

- Has a very good sense of humour for age (appreciates wit/irony/metaphor, etc.)

A child showing most of the above characteristics but not those asterisked is potentially a gifted child who is underachieving educationally.

2. List compiled by teachers during professional development session

- Possesses extensive general knowledge

- Has quick mastery and recall of information

- Has exceptional curiosity

- Asks many provocative and/or searching questions

- Shows good insight into cause–effect relationships

- Easily grasps underlying principles and needs the minimum of explanation

- Quickly makes generalisations

- Often sees unusual rather than conventional relationships

- Jumps stages in learning

- Leaps from the concrete to the abstract

- Is a keen and alert observer

- Sees greater significance in a story or film

- When interested becomes absorbed

- Is persistent in seeking task completion

- Is more than usually interested in 'adult' problems such as religion, politics, etc.

- Displays intellectual playfulness: fantasises, imagines, manipulates ideas

- Is concerned to adapt and improve institutions, objects, systems

- Has a keen sense of humour; sees humour in the unusual

- Appreciates verbal puns, cartoons, jokes, etc.

- Criticises constructively

- Is unwilling to accept authoritarian pronouncements without critical examination

- Mental speed faster than physical capabilities

- Prefers to talk rather than write

- Daydreams

- Reluctant to practise skills already mastered

- Reads rapidly and retains what is read

- Has advanced understanding and use of language

- Shows sensitivity

- Shows empathy towards others

- Sees the problem quickly and takes the initiative.

3. Characteristics of gifted learners in the classroom

- *Memory and knowledge*: they know more, they know what they know better and they can use it more effectively.

- *Self-regulation*: they guide and monitor their own thinking on task.

- *Speed of thought processes*: they spend longer on planning but arrive at answers more quickly. Their solutions are often shorter and/or more abstract, like those of experts.

- *Problem presentation and categorisation*: they extend working beyond the information given, identifying missing information, excluding irrelevance and grasping the essentials of the task more quickly.

- *Procedural knowledge*: they organise their approaches to problem-solving and are flexible in switching approaches where necessary.

- *Flexibility*: they are able to draw inferences, see alternative configurations and adopt alternative strategies.

- *Curiosity*: they ask questions, play with ideas, initiate projects, invent approaches.

- *Preference for complexity*: they increase the complexity and elaborate on tasks to increase interest.

4. Giftedness and creativity

(A) Fluency:

- Expressiveness

- Spontaneous flow of ideas

- Sees many connections.

(Continued)

(Continued)

(B) Flexibility:

- Tendency to experiment freely with ideas and subjects, media, materials and techniques
- Facility for solving problems using non-traditional or innovative methods
- Aptitude for viewing/approaching work from a different perspective
- Tolerance of ambiguity and conflict
- Ability to adapt from one situation or medium to another.

(C) Originality:

- High degree of imagination; ability to image clearly
- Freedom to adapt away from given stimuli
- Tendency to experiment as opposed to adopting preconceived solutions.

(D) Elaboration:

- Use of many elements
- Facility for 'piggybacking'/'hitchhiking' on from (as opposed to copying) the ideas of others; to develop them further.

5. Characteristics of AG&T underachievers

- Bored and restless
- Low self-esteem
- Fluent orally but poor in written work
- Friendly with older children and adults
- Confused about their learning, behaviour and future development
- Absorbed in a private world
- Excessively self-critical, anxious and may feel rejected by family
- Find failure in others, materials, systems, etc. to excuse/justify their behaviour
- Possibly emotionally unstable
- Hostile towards authority
- Quick thinking
- Don't know how to learn academically
- Aspirations too low for aptitudes
- Don't set own goals, relying on teacher for decisions
- Don't think ahead
- Poor performance in tests but asking creative, searching questions
- Thinking in abstract terms

- Enjoying playing with language
- High-level work has deteriorated over time
- Can be inventive in response to open-ended questions
- Can be creative and/or persevering when motivated.

Step Two: Produce a school-based list combining generic indicators with any issues that audit and review have shown to be relevant to the school (e.g. learning styles, underachievement, language development, etc.). Most generic characteristics can be adopted/adapted from these or other checklists. Highlight the relevant statements, add those that address local concerns and, from Step One, compile a checklist with an approach that best fits the school's purpose. Remember that different phases of education raise particular questions of identification (45 minutes).

Phase	Identification issues and questions
Early Years	Is precociousness the same as giftedness? Does limited skill development (e.g. reading or writing) mean not gifted? Is easily bored and/or disruptive always a sign of lack of challenge? Is an emotionally immature but academically advanced child AG&T?
Primary	Does taking fewer steps and quick work mean independent learner? Are abstract thought, open-ended enquiry and creativity key indicators? What does the inability to cope with failure and/or take risks suggest? Are low levels of self-esteem compatible with AG&T and if so why? Does chronological age matter when identifying mental age?
Secondary	Can 'negative' traits such as non-conformity, anti-authoritarianism and low motivation be seen as indices of high ability? What links a sense of humour, divergent thinking and creativity? What are the signs of growing self-determination, intellectual curiosity, concentration and developing passion in a chosen field? Is AG&T revealed most clearly when working with peers of similar ability?

Step Three: When the school checklist has been agreed, the final step is to use the criteria to inform any pupil profiling or tracking process that may contribute to the identification and nomination of a pupil for the AG&T register. Clearly,

(Continued)

(Continued)

identification will need to take account of measured attainment, but it should also allow for the varied and complex patterns of underachievement to which AG&T children are subject. Factors behind this include: lack of self-confidence; 'learned' patterns of low-level application; the conscious or unconscious desire to conform; the desire to avoid extra work; low expectations among parents and/or teachers; and environmental/cultural factors working against assigning value to education or study. The aim is to produce a simple tick-box pro forma to provide a learning overview when considering pupils for inclusion within the AG&T provision (up to 60 minutes). Figure 3.3 provides a model on which such a development might be based.

Name . . . .   Sex . . . . DoB . . . . Group . . . .

Curriculum/Test outcomes (NB asterisk marks in top 5% nationally)

Current Curriculum/Teacher Assessment Level(s)

Characteristic		Below Average	Average	Good	Excellent
Skills	Reading				
	Writing				
	Number				
Development	Language				
	Vocabulary				
	Emotional/ Social				
Thinking	Reasoning				
	Abstraction				
	Creativity				
Aptitude for Learning	Application				
	Concentration				
	Curiosity and Questioning				
Class work	Routine tasks				
	Collaboration				

Figure 3.3

Subject-specific characteristics

The previous chapter outlined how many – indeed most – individuals are not generally gifted but specifically so. This means that alongside generic characteristics it is also necessary to identify the nature of high performance in discrete academic areas and subject-specific specialisms. It is beyond the scope of this book to address fully the nature of excellence in each curriculum area, but the recommendation is that schools do exactly that. Understanding the skills and competencies that define excellence in subject-specific terms is not only an important factor in identifying ability but it also allows subject teachers to lead learners towards high achievement and to understand what has to be done to secure the highest levels. For this reason subject coordinators and academic departments need to replicate school policy at subject level to define the nature of excellence in their area for that age group, establish identification/assessment procedures to help recognise it when it arises and feed that information into the whole-school system.

Again, checklists can prove useful in this endeavour. A scrutiny of previous attempts to formulate the underlying competencies of high achievement can provide subject specialists with a framework for developing their own school-based checklists. Most mathematics checklists, for example, tend to see excellent practice characterised by:

- Swiftness in reasoning in relation to problem-solving

- The ability to think abstractly, reason analytically and generalise broadly

- The ability to perceive mathematical patterns, structures and relationships

- Flexibility in thinking/searching for alternative solutions

- A strong task-commitment for work in mathematics.

While such an approach can provide a useful categorisation of competencies for identification purposes, it must be remembered that even the most gifted youngsters are only working towards the established practice of adult experts. In this sense, subject specialists may find that curriculum-based formulations of progression (such as the 10-level descriptors charting progression in all English National Curriculum subjects) provide a more 'teacherly' source of information about the evolving competencies required within the range of performance assessed up to GCSE A*. From such information it is possible to extrapolate the range of characteristics shown by high-attaining pupils in a subject across the relevant age-range of the cohort.

English	Mathematics	Science
Creative flair	Understands ideas easily	Imaginative in science
Coherent expression	Systematic & accurate	Scientific hobbies
Elaborates/organises	Analytical	Curiosity about nature
Stamina & perseverance	Logical	Enjoys facts and theories
Communicative	Makes connections	Searches for deeper truths
Metaphorical	Sees patterns	Inquisitive about how/why
Sensitive to style/audience	Applies knowledge	Hypothesises & speculates
Elegant expression	Creative problem-solving	Uses different strategies
Reasoned argument	Question-finding	Methodical thinking
Awareness of language		Objective argument

An alternative approach is for subject areas to determine in advance what high performance in particular topics, units of work or assessment opportunities should look like. Again, this approach combines opportunities for identification with clear frameworks for teachers and learners, as this example from a Y3 geography scheme of work for local area study illustrates:

> An exceptionally able pupil expresses views confidently about attractive and unattractive environmental and physical features (e.g. the impact of traffic on the environment). S/he suggests improvements and sees how these may affect different people. S/he uses appropriate vocabulary to reveal understanding of how geographical features will differ between localities. Work is illustrated with maps and diagrams. S/he is able to relate locations to maps accurately, and provides directions between places, using terms correctly. When researching information, s/he poses relevant questions, suggests ways of obtaining answers and expresses this with confidence. His/her work will consistently demonstrate achievement well above expected levels.

One vitally important feature of approaching identification from the point of view of evaluating the quality of pupils' response against agreed criteria for excellence in any given piece of work is the opportunity it provides for schools and individual teachers to evaluate their own practice by assessing the impact of that practice on pupils' achievement. Where, for example, work set by teachers fails to elicit the type of high achievement hoped for, then this implies the need to review and adapt current schemes of work/preferred pedagogic approaches to ensure that they are challenging in the ways required to produce the desired higher order response. Once again, teachers need to be constantly aware that the ongoing loop connecting pedagogic practice, assessment and ongoing improvement relates not only to pupil outcomes but also to the quality of provision made available by teachers.

> ### Activity
>
> In subject-specific pairs or groups, identify a current topic for a particular year group, preferably one used for summative assessment purposes. Use checklists and/or level descriptors plus subject knowledge to agree what exceptional performance in the unit of work would look like. Then:
>
> - Produce a short descriptor in continuous prose or bullet points to establish the criteria for high attainment in this topic
>
> - Discuss how teachers might work best to secure these outcomes and draw up a suggested list of key interventions intended to promote a high quality response
>
> - Develop a pupil-friendly method (e.g. simple target-sheet, model response, preliminary PowerPoint, concept map, etc.) to mediate the topic with pupils in a way that makes clear to them what a very good response should contain.
>
> This activity can be addressed in a professional development session (in total 75–90 minutes) or be seen as an ongoing task to build AG&T identification and assessment materials into all subject-specific schemes of work.

What are the learning needs of AG&T pupils?

Personalisation requires teachers to understand the individual learning needs of pupils and pupils to have ownership of their obligations and opportunities to succeed as learners. Although AG&T learners do not necessarily have the most urgent difficulties, there are a number of characteristic problems that some youngsters encounter as a consequence of their high ability, including:

- Difficulties in relating to less perceptive peers, resulting in social isolation

- Frustration that their skills (e.g. drawing) do not match their understanding

- Impatience, anger or moodiness when faced with unaccustomed failure

- A preference for older or adult company, causing strained relationships

- Deep interest in areas of strength but a tendency to reject weaker subjects

- Mimicking achievement and behaviour of weaker peers to gain approval

- Arrogance or dismissiveness towards those with conflicting points of view.

While these behaviours can help to identify AG&T pupils, they can also be misleading. Relationship difficulties, mood-management issues and underachievement can also occur without giftedness as the cause. This is one reason why the link between identification and provision is key. If pupils are to be identified as AG&T on the basis of pastoral and/or academic difficulties, then a teacher's response to the problem(s) needs to be of the sort to disentangle the positive aspects of the learner's capabilities from their more negative consequences. These potentially murky waters can be clarified by recourse to the entitlements of AG&T pupils as learners. These include the following:

The need to be challenged

Underattainment can be an acquired habit of mind caused by lack of domestic stimulation/encouragement and/or learned classroom behaviours resulting from low expectations, uninspiring tasks, frustrating, unnecessarily repetitious, routines and the unavailability of any intellectual incentive to work through core material towards higher order extension and enrichment opportunities. Able, gifted and talented pupils are entitled to work at a level appropriate to their ability rather than one defined by a 'catch-all' task.

The right to develop in the round

There is a tendency for the gifted in one area (say mathematics) to neglect or even disparage other academic or social aspects of education that provide them with a less immediate sense of satisfaction and achievement. Younger children, for example, may grow impatient with the laboriousness of basic skill acquisition and so fail to establish a secure basis for future learning. Schools should be wary of any inclination to concentrate excessively on areas of ability at the expense of general academic and social development.

The need for social integration

All AG&T pupils, especially those with exceptional abilities, need to be at ease among their peers. Equally, however, they benefit greatly from spending time in the company of like-minded learners who are able to reduce the sense of isolation experienced by many gifted children. Achieving this balance of integration for all while supporting difference is a major challenge for schools, but an important one to achieve if AG&T learners are to maintain a sense of self-actualisation and yet learn to respect the contributions and value of others.

Home/school partnerships

Raising gifted children can be difficult. Some carers interpret the relentless curiosity, limited sleep patterns, intellectual energy and precocity of pre-school children as naughtiness and this negativity can colour attitudes towards school. Children of a more introverted cast of mind whose potential is ignored can become introspective and appear to be indifferent, uninterested and of low ability. Other, more aspirational, parents can make their children anxious or develop a sense of grievance about the unreasonable and inequitable demands placed on them.

Alternatively, some youngsters are treated at their intellectual rather than their emotional level, which can make for unhappy and confused children who fit in poorly at school. For these and other reasons any parental partnerships and pupil mentoring schemes available should not automatically exclude more able learners.

The right to experience joy in learning

Some AG&T children can be overwhelmed and made miserable by the high expectations placed on them. All learners need time to experiment with less formal, more creative, more transitional pieces of work which allow ideas and skills to develop away from the constant pressure to attain at the highest level of accomplishment. A classroom culture of experimentation and preparation, of creativity and joy in learning is likely to lead towards more balanced, successful, learners than a pressurised determination on the part of schools to keep the noses of their most able firmly fixed to the grindstone.

The concluding focus on learning needs is significant. It is by understanding and identifying the needs of the gifted that we will make the crucial link between identification and provision. Knowing what children need to become successful learners is the first step towards knowing what provision must be put in place to meet those needs. Without this understanding we will not develop a suitably personalised approach to the AG&T cohort. Chapter 4 addresses the issue of whole-school provision in support of AG&T learners. Such provision is key to securing the inclusive practices necessary to allow high achievement to flourish within the organisation as a whole. It is also, of course, such provision which scaffolds and supports individual teachers in their attempt to deliver effective classroom challenge. In-class provision is the focus of Chapter 5.

Summary

Some key points and suggestions have been made in this chapter in relation to identifying AG&T learners.

- There is an iceberg effect with AG&T populations which suggests that for all those identifiable through test outcomes there will be more whose potential is less clearly realised.

- Teacher identification/nomination is the most reliable means of recognising unrealised or obscure ability given appropriate training.

- Pupil response to work designed to reveal AG&T performance is a key assessment tool to use in identifying potential.

Whole-school provision for AG&T

> ## Issues of whole-school provision under discussion include:
>
> - **The evaluation of the learning environment**
> - **Cross-curricular planning in support of creative learning**
> - **Auditing the impact of curriculum support initiatives for the more able**
> - **The role of school leadership in embedding personalised learning practices for AG&T pupils**
> - **Using AG&T mentors as a part of a coordinated learning support programme.**

This chapter looks at provision for AG&T learners at the whole-school level. Accordingly, it may be read as a personal guide in support of good practice or as providing support for a wider programme of institutional audit and change. As throughout the book, the emphasis is on supporting and structuring professional development opportunities for organisations developing whole-school provision for their AG&T cohort.

Activity

The photocopiable form (Figure 4.1) raises a number of key questions about the overall learning climate in your school or setting as it relates to AG&T learners. The aim is to give an honest response to each statement rating your current provision in relation to each question on the scale one to five, with five indicating a very strong or fully secure aspect. The positive/negative boxes are to make a note of any particularly effective element(s) of current provision and any key area(s) for attention and improvement.

Where this questionnaire can be completed by all staff (working in pairs), by subject area or year-group teams or by steering group members, the collated responses can contribute to an audit of whole-school provision for AG&T learners. Areas to emerge as clearly in need of improvement can be included in the AG&T improvement plan.

Whole-school learning environment questions	Score 1–5	Positive	Negative
Does the rewards system recognise and celebrate all areas of outstanding endeavour equally? Is outstanding work in all academic areas given the same degree of reward and recognition as, for example, sports and music?			
Does assessment for learning policy and practice routinely provide even the most able pupils with clear and comprehensible advice and personalised targets on how to improve?			
Do pupils have the opportunity to develop/extend opportunities for student voice into areas of evaluation of provision and subsequent mapping/developing/negotiating appropriate work?			
Does display around the school and in classrooms show pupils that learning and high achievement are highly valued and celebrated?			
Is hard work rewarded and praised or is it simply expected?			
Is independence in learning and thinking actively encouraged and supported?			
Do AG&T pupils operate in a secure environment where they feel happy to display ability and to take risks without fear of reprisal or ridicule?			
Do AG&T pupils experience sufficient challenge to the point of finding work difficult (sometimes to the point of failure)?			
Are AG&T pupils able to relax and/or be allowed the latitude and freedom of expression to experience joy in learning?			
Are pupils allowed to experience exciting intellectual discussion, debate and enquiry, both in and beyond the classroom?			
Do learning opportunities recognise the range of learning styles?			
Are pupils encouraged to ask searching questions secure in the knowledge that they will be given a considered response?			
Is experimentation and 'having a go' valued and encouraged as conspicuously as 'getting it right?'			
Do teachers expect, plan for and encourage excellence as opposed to merely competence?			
Are AG&T pupils, even the exceptionally gifted, recognised as individuals with particular strengths and weaknesses as learners?			

Figure 4.1 Whole-school learning environment questions

Photocopiable:

Teaching Able, Gifted and Talented Children © Clive Tunnicliffe 2010 (SAGE)

An additional audit of whole-school educational practice can provide an overall picture of provision (and the variations in approach experienced by pupils across the curriculum). The following 10 questions relating to individual classroom practice may be used in the same way as the whole-school questions to arrive at an evaluation of the quality of provision for AG&T learners made by particular practitioners, discrete subject areas and, when examined cumulatively, the teaching staff generally:

1. Do you prepare materials to extend, stretch and stimulate AG&T learners?

2. Are they kept fully and meaningfully occupied?

3. Once routine work is finished does extension work motivate and excite rather than merely require additional labour?

4. Do you demand quality before quantity?

5. Do you give them an equal amount of your time?

6. Do you promote pupil evaluation of their learning so that they work with you in developing/co-constructing their own flexible learning pathways?

7. Are you providing as many open-ended situations as possible?

8. Do you have plenty of supplementary resource materials available for their use?

9. Are you encouraging depth, breadth and independence of thought?

10. Do you set them goals/targets beyond the level you expect of others based on your assessment of learning need?

While any school or setting will respond to these questions in terms that are linked to its context and circumstances, the following general pointers towards good practice should help inform any encapsulation of individual, departmental or whole-school improvement planning on the topic of developing an effective AG&T learning environment or classroom ethos:

• The display of pupil's work should promote and celebrate achievement at all levels of attainment, including the highest.

• Models of best practice should be displayed which provide stimulation and scaffolds for emulation for the highest attainers as well as those supporting the less able.

• Opportunities for pupils to reflect on and assess/develop their own learning should be routinely available withing normal classroom provision.

- Materials/learning opportunities should be made available within the classroom to support early finishers and provide additional intellectual challenge (e.g. enrichment corners/boxes, puzzles and thinking challenges, challenge cards, computer programs to extend learning, etc.).

- Reward systems (such as attractive merit point charts or interactive and exciting compilation formats – e.g. filling bottles with reward tokens) should be prominently displayed and positively referred to in classrooms, pastoral time, assemblies and elsewhere.

- Vocabulary and other academic prompts displayed to support work in the classroom should provide sufficient range to support and encourage children of all abilities to extend the repertoire of words/concepts incorporated in their work.

Emerging whole-school planning and development issues

Cross-curricular engagement

However effectively individual teachers provide for their most able learners in the classroom, whole-school planning needs to ensure that the curriculum in its entirety actively supports continuity and progression in learning for all pupils. Of course, in the UK the various National Curriculum schemes of work (and associated National Strategy Frameworks for Learning) support the quest for breadth, balance and relevance in learning. Many schools, however, particularly in the primary sector have expressed the view that teaching in separate subject areas promotes linear learning styles and inhibits pupils' capacity to make connections between the different areas of their learning.

While the consensus view (e.g. expressed by Jim Rose in the 2009 UK White Paper, *Your Child, Your School, Our Future* (DCSF, 2009) on the primary curriculum) is that the core areas of literacy, numeracy and ICT should be taught in subject-specific blocks, there are significant gains to be made by ensuring that learners are able to make effective connections between subjects. Clearly, facilitating the making of connections in pursuit of 'joined-up learning' is aligned to the desire to devise a more creative curriculum in so far as creativity itself draws on the perception of links between disparate objects or areas of experience. In this sense, a whole-school initiative in which areas of learning are presented through common themes or topics can be effective in supporting AG&T learners in developing creative thinking, independence in learning and higher-order understanding.

A problem traditionally associated with this type of creative curriculum planning, however, is that common topics can fail to yield the academic rigour necessary to meet all learning entitlements across all of the subject areas touched on by the combined topic. To combat this tendency a number of initiatives have endeavoured to ensure rigour is maintained by carefully mapping out all of the specified learning criteria in all of the curriculum strands and matching them against planned activities within the chosen topic. Even in such cases where learning criteria have been carefully plotted across the planned activities, however, it is still possible to provide a joined-up learning experience which, in itself, does not promote the higher order engagements with the material which are necessary to stimulate critical and creative thinking for all pupils and provide appropriate challenge for the most able.

If it is to be an appropriate method of meeting the needs of all learners then cross-curricular or multidisciplinary planning needs to place emphasis on pedagogic approach as well as on meeting the required learning criteria. In this way, creative curriculum planning will support creativity in helping pupils make connections across their learning, and will also actively promote the higher order thinking skills necessary for high level engagement with any topic (see Figure 4.2).

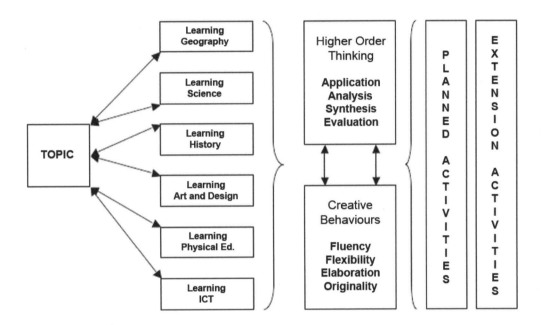

Figure 4.2 Cross-curricular planning for higher level learning

Clearly, national learning criteria and given skills-based learning objectives are subject to review and modification as governments and priorities change over time. It is the role of school leadership, however, to ensure that curriculum planning unites both the appropriate learning objectives with pedagogic approaches proven to maximise challenge and maintain academic rigour for all learners.

Chapter 5 on classroom provision concludes with a model of an approach to cross-curricular planning to be undertaken by individual practitioners and/or year-group planning teams. To ensure that this development work in settings is undertaken systematically, however, it will be necessary for curriculum leaders to ensure that information and advice is collected and disseminated to planning teams *in situ* to ensure that their work is informed by school-based and other professional evidence of teaching strategies which have been proven to maximise impact on pupils' development as creative, independent learners.

Evaluating impact and equality

Current perception of best practice in the UK envisages schools and settings undertaking rigorous self-evaluation to identify the effectiveness of their own performance in improving outcomes for their users (e.g. download *Ofsted Inspects* from www.ofsted.gov.uk/Ofsted-home/Forms-and-guidance). Clearly, the self-evaluation needs to take into account the hard data available around pupil performance in a similar manner to that modelled in Chapter 2 in the section on data analysis and whole-school audit. In terms of monitoring equality, however, it is necessary to be more precise in tracking pupil performance than merely identifying trends in pupil achievement (or progress) and attainment (measured standards) between gender alignment in three broad ability bands.

Drawing on school performance analysis programs (such as Pupil Achievement Tracker (www.standards.dfes.gov.uk/performance/pat/) allows schools to identify not only broad patterns in performance but to isolate differences in outcomes between more precisely targeted pupil groups/designations (e.g. more able African Caribbean boys) and between the achievement and attainment of individual pupils (e.g. each pupil identified as exceptionally able). Group-specific or individual monitoring of this sort to reveal a personalised performance profile (so, for example, revealing a youngster's pattern of attainment in all assessment questions across the core curriculum areas) or a distinct trend in underachievement affecting one but not other pupil groupings is of huge benefit to schools in identifying areas of success, of relative weakness and in targeting areas for future intervention and resource allocation. At a personalised level such detailed monitoring can also be extremely useful information for mentors and/or tutors to share with AG&T youngsters and their parents as a way of establishing targets for improvement, extending responsibility for that improvement to the learner and his/her family, and encouraging students to discuss, and thus contribute to, the school's understanding of successful and less successful learning and teaching strategies.

Such analyses are key to a school's understanding of its provision for AG&T. Not only do they provide evidence of pupil performance, but, in some ways more crucially, they provide evidence of the impact of the current measures being taken to meet the learning needs of that particular group or individual. Assessing impact, however, requires more than data analysis, even individualised analysis. If a school is successful in identifying, say, variations in attainment among AG&T individuals, this information can provide the starting point for a more qualitative analysis of factors underlying such discrepancies and, from this, lead towards a clearer institutional understanding of provision which is having a positive impact on learners and that which is less successful in supporting effective progress. In this case the self-evaluation of data should be followed by active research into the causes of the identified statistical phenomena. Such research may involve:

- Classroom observations undertaken in particularly successful subject areas/classes as a way of identifying the strategies/activities producing the greatest impact

- Individual or target pupil tracking across different curriculum areas to identify practices responsible for producing a greater and lesser impact on learning

- Discussions with pupils and parents to obtain and act upon users' perceptions of the relative impact of teaching styles on learning and progress

- Work scrutiny activities to identify those approaches which produce the greatest impact on either a group or a focus individual's performance

- The examination of target elements of provision (e.g. after-school clubs) to ascertain their impact on students in terms of numbers involved, perceived outcomes, equality of opportunity, measured gains and value for money/effectiveness when compared with alternative provision (e.g. the library study skills course).

While the responsibility for organising and disseminating audit of this type lies with school leadership, it is important that the outcomes of such evaluations are made available to individual staff, planning groups or subject teams as a springboard for their own improvements/curriculum developments drawing on the evidence of impact revealed through action research. For example, a staff development day on equality of provision for the more able could present case studies for consideration and discussion of:

- A record of an individual's (or of contrasting individuals') school week in terms of required activity, challenge, engagement, repetition, patterns of attainment and personal attitudes/feelings relating to the work required

- Extracts from students' work revealing significant patterns of achievement in relation to types of activity

- Transcripts of conversations with AG&T students commenting and reflecting on their preferences and difficulties in terms of the taught curriculum

- Pieces of set work which evidence has found to be particularly challenging and/or productive in terms of their impact on AG&T outcomes.

Clearly, such opportunities for teaching staff to consider the elements of provision already found to maximise learning in the school are vital in isolating areas of proven success to build on when modifying and improving current schemes of work from the point of view of AG&T provision. When this information is combined with the type of generic recommendations discussed in Chapter 5, leadership may genuinely be felt to be effectively scaffolding the development of more focused strategies for supporting AG&T within individual classrooms. In addition, the making available of learning profiles of individual (possibly exceptionally able) youngsters to all staff will impact positively on the development of personalised learning across the school.

Personalised learning for AG&T

However successfully schools and settings are able to deliver an open-ended, effectively mixed-ability curriculum offer, it will always be necessary to support individual learners individually; particularly at either end of the ability range where difficulties can arise relating to the atypicality of the learner's needs.

As we've seen, assessment for learning practice is a key factor distinguishing personalisation from differentiation. In this context, pupils are provided with information through the processes of assessment (e.g. through formative marking procedures, self-assessment and self-evaluation, academic feedback, pupil-level target-setting strategies, academic mentoring, academic monitoring, pastoral counselling, etc.) which gives them a clear understanding of their individual strengths and weaknesses as learners and – crucially – makes clear what they must do to improve. For all pupils, this clarity provides an important measure of understanding about their ongoing progression as learners and what they need to do to realise their full potential. For AG&T pupils, whose accomplishments are often already equal to the maximum expectations of a generic classroom task, it is even more important to be given personal guidance or direction regarding individual improvements which would provide both a genuine challenge and a realistic line of progression. Clearly, self-evaluation of learning needs and the construction (or – in collaboration with teachers – the co-construction) of appropriate curriculum challenge is an important feature of effective provision for the most able if they are to develop as effectively independent learners.

The key to personalisation, therefore, is to provide pupils with a growing understanding and ownership of their own strengths and weaknesses as learners; their own opportunities and responsibilities to themselves as they strive to make the most of their potential for success. Clearly, as young people pass through the school system there are increasing opportunities for teachers to use the electronic means of mapping patterns of achievement in standardised assessments as a way of prompting youngsters to reflect on their own detailed breakdown of relative accomplishment across subject areas, within particular subjects and even in response to particular types of questions. Further to secure the impact of such an approach, however, the teacher needs to be able to augment the raw analysis of data with an accurate diagnosis of the pupil's strengths, weaknesses and preferences as a learner and to discuss these in a way the child can understand, take ownership of and act upon.

Personalisation as a concept is still in the process of professional assimilation and there are many competing claims for incorporation in an overall definition of the term. Alongside assessment for learning practice, interest is being focused on the potential of twenty-first-century technology to guarantee learners a more personalised experience of education. Accordingly, personalisation may be felt to involve:

• The *thinking curriculum* in which thinking skills are explicitly taught as a way of giving individuals the cerebral abilities to engage with the academic curriculum in a more personally productive manner

- An understanding of *learning styles* and the impact of preferred learning styles on individual engagement and accomplishment in particular tasks

- *Learning to learn* which involves the metacognitive awareness among teachers and pupils of learning processes and the best way(s) for individuals to learn

- *Mentoring* whereby individuals are provided with support, metacognitive awareness and feedback about their progress and targets as learners

- *Individualised learning* programmes established or accessed to meet the specific requirements of particular pupils, including the exceptionally able

- *Personal learning plans* which for AG&T pupils would set out the broad objectives and avenues of support or improvement open to targeted individuals

- *Independent learning skills* leading towards more autonomous learning in which pupils develop and evaluate their own learning within an environment in which *student-led learning* is given active encouragement

- Individually targeted *ICT applications* and the deployment of *virtual learning environments (VLEs)* to tailor learning experiences to individual developmental need.

Whatever the future holds for schools in terms of VLEs, it is clear that for the time being, personalisation is predicated on a good understanding of learning styles and capabilities on the part of both teachers and learners. Typing 'learning styles' into an internet search engine reveals a great number of competing formulations of types of learning style, ranging from large numbers of highly specific learning approaches to small numbers of generic learning preferences. It also provides access to a number of online tests designed to reveal a pupil's preferred and least favoured learning style. A typical model of learners' differing competencies and preferences envisages four broad styles of learning, as shown in Figure 4.3.

Teachers and learners armed with appropriate information about preferred learning styles are then able to ensure that attention is given to developing areas of relative weakness while recognising – and planning for – the fact that the highest achievement for any individual will arise when set tasks involve working within the preferred style(s). So visual learners will excel in the use of images and visualisation; art and drawing; maps, charts and diagrams; pattern work, text marking strategies using coloured annotations and all forms of mind-mapping and other graphical information techniques. Kinaesthetic learners will achieve more highly when their work involves the possibility of movement, physical demonstrations and mnemonics; manipulating and touching materials and hands-on, preferably outdoor activity. Auditory learners thrive when being required to verbalise problems; through phonic-based work and through all forms of aural input. Logical learners enjoy experimentation and recording; computer programs/games; puzzles and all forms of deductive reasoning challenges; and non-fiction materials.

Visual learners	Auditory learners
• like demonstrations • learn through descriptions • often use lists • have good sight recognition • show developed imaginations • are distracted by movement or action • tend to be unaware of noise. Students who are not visual often read a page and then realise they don't know what they have read.	• like the teacher to provide verbal instructions • find it easy to learn by listening • enjoy dialogues, discussions and plays • offer remember names but forget faces • solve problems by talking them out • are easily distracted by noise • often do best using recorded books. Students who are not auditory find it difficult to concentrate or listen for long periods. They will often tune out what is being said or find it hard to stay with the speaker.
Kinaesthetic learners	**Logical learners**
• often do best when they are involved or active • may have high energy levels • think and learn best while moving • can lose much of what is said during verbal input • have problems concentrating when asked to sit and read • prefer to do rather than watch or listen. Non-kinaesthetic learners rarely get involved in action-oriented activities. They would rather drive than walk. They would prefer not to participate and to watch.	• think conceptually • like to explore patterns and relationships • enjoy puzzles and seeing how things work • like routine and consistency • are capable of highly abstract forms of logical thinking at early age • do mental arithmetic easily • enjoy strategy games, ICT and experiments • create own designs to build with blocks, etc. Non-logical learners are often not so good at creative activities and may find difficulty working imaginatively.

Figure 4.3 Styles of learning

In this sense learning styles are closely related to Howard Gardner's (1983, 2006) concept of multiple intelligences, where the various domains of mental functioning or ability correspond to preferences which both reveal themselves in classroom responses and also provide evidence of an individual's overall profile as a learner – see Table 4.1.

This information is key to the learning to learn aspect of personalisation. Where pupils understand the processes of learning and how their personal predispositions figure across the spectrum of learning styles or domains they are able to draw on specific study skill techniques to match their own areas of comfort and also to develop their expertise as learners in areas that lie outside their comfort zone.

Developing competencies that are not naturally amenable is an important area of development for many AG&T learners. For those individuals with the potential to achieve highly in education and in career progression, it is important that the impulse to specialise or concentrate excessively on areas and approaches that provide the maximum psychological gratification is challenged to the extent that expertise in a wide range of study skills and disciplines can be acquired. In this sense personalisation for AG&T may also mean supporting learners through incompatible or inimical areas of the curriculum. It can mean helping youngsters who are used to success cope with the frustrations and failures that even the most gifted individuals will encounter during their professional lives.

This is an area in which academic mentoring can be of particular help in helping AG&T pupils develop an appropriate repertoire of learning skills and personal abilities to match the demands of a fully-rounded educational programme. Schools and settings seeking to develop personalised approaches may find the model set out in Figure 4.4 useful as a means of evaluating current practice and highlighting areas for future development, both generally and for AG&T learners particularly.

Table 4.1 Multiple intelligence characteristics

Linguistic	*Logical-mathematical*	*Visual-spatial*
Sensitive to patterns	Likes abstract thinking	Thinks in pictures
Orderly	Likes being precise	Creates mental images
Systematic	Enjoys counting	Uses metaphor
Ability to reason	Likes being organised	Has sense of gestalt
Likes to listen	Uses logical structure	Likes art, drawing, painting
Likes to read	Enjoys computers	sculpting
Likes to write	Enjoys problem-solving	Easily reads maps, charts
Spells easily	Enjoys experimenting in a	diagrams
Likes word games	logical way	Remembers with pictures
Has good memory for trivia	Prefers orderly note-taking	Has good colour sense

Bodily kinaesthetic	*Musical*
Exceptional control of body	Sensitive to pitch, rhythm and timbre
Good timing	Sensitive to emotional power of music
Trained responses	Sensitive to complex organisation of music
Good reflexes	May be deeply spiritual
Learns best by moving	
Enjoys sports and acting	
Remembers action rather than words	
Plays around with objects while listening	
Fidgety if there are few breaks	
Mechanically minded	

Intrapersonal or intuitive	*Interpersonal or social*
Self-knowledge	Negotiates well
Sensitivity to one's own values	Relates well, mixes well
Deeply aware of one's own feelings	Able to read others' intentions
Has well developed sense of self	Enjoys being with people
Intuitive ability	Communicates well, sometimes manipulates
Self-motivated	Enjoys group activities
Deeply aware of own strengths/weaknesses	Likes to mediate disputes
Very private person	Likes to cooperate
Wants to be different from mainstream	'Reads' social situations well

	Pupil Voice	AG&T Mentor	ICT and tech	ILP* for AG&T	PLP** for AG&T	Self-Ass't/ Eval	Over-all mark	Areas to develop
Assessment for learning								
Learning to learn								
Curriculum, relevance and flexibility								
Organisational/ staffing safeguards								
Thinking curriculum								

* ILP = Individualised Learning Programmes
** PLP = Personal Learning Plans

Figure 4.4 Matrix model for evaluating whole-school provision

The aim of this matrix approach is to evaluate (from one to five with one as fully secure and five as not yet in place) the current level of personalised support for AG&T pupils as part of an integrated whole-school approach. The matrix helps to visualise the connectedness of particular aspects of provision across five key areas of personalised support. So, for example, if the school does have an AG&T mentor then this factor reflects positively in the organisational/staffing safeguards box. If, however, the mentor's work is poorly linked to work being developed on assessment for learning then this will reflect negatively in the corresponding box, thereby indicating an area of provision for future development within the personalisation agenda.

Clearly the model can be freely adapted/adopted for academic departments, subject areas or individual practitioners to evaluate their current practice. The approach is also a useful starting point for supporting discussion with particular pupils as a way of structuring a dialogue around self-evaluation, learning to learn and a negotiated curriculum for AG&T youngsters. An appropriate framework for learning mentors or academic target-setting/learning to learn discussions might include the headings suggested as prompts for an ongoing dialogue or support schedule in the accompanying AG&T Mentor Checklist and Discussion Pro Forma (Figure 4.5).

As the pro forma for mentors suggests, discussions with AG&T pupils around some or all (depending on age, time allocation, etc.) of the issues impacting on personalised learning and support should ensure that:

• Information relating to marking and other assessments by academic teachers should be communicated to the mentor

AG&T Mentor Checklist and Discussion Pro forma

	Areas for discussion		
	General learning improvements	Academic areas	Child-centred advice and/or targets
Assessment for learning **Improvement targets**			
Peer assessment			
Self-assessment			
Learning to learn **Learning styles**			
Study skills			
Thinking skills			
Curriculum flexibility and relevance **Personal learning plans**			
Individualised learning programmes			
ICT/VLE			
Beyond the classroom **Partnerships (e.g. NACE)**			
Home/school links			
Extra-curricular			
Overview			

Figure 4.5

- Opportunities for pupils – and parents – to comment on and help develop current provision (e.g. through self-assessment and evaluation) are also built into the overall evaluation and development of provision

- Care is taken, particularly with younger learners, to establish objectives/targets for future improvement in a language/format that the pupil can understand and agree to act upon.

Ultimately, the AG&T cohort in any setting is more likely than many other pupil groups to act upon and benefit from advice and support provided. This is not to say, however, that the support is either not required or can be skimped on. Personalisation is a powerful idea guaranteeing individual support for all learners both within and beyond the taught curriculum. For AG&T learners it acts both as a safeguard to guarantee learning entitlements and progression and also as a recognition that for many able learners the support provided by the school in the new technological age can extend beyond the walls of the setting and reach out into the wider worlds of educational opportunity that now exist. More attention will be given to this extended community and virtual landscape of opportunity in Chapter 5. It is, however, to the role of the teacher in the classroom that the discussion of provision now turns.

To think about

- What is/are the most pressing area(s) of improvement necessary for school systems to support AG&T more effectively?

- How will desired improvements be planned and implemented?

- How effective is current practice around assessment for learning and learning to learn in supporting personalised learning objectives for AG&T?

Summary

Some key points have been made in this chapter relating to whole-school provision.

- The overall learning environment should anticipate, celebrate and reward high achievement.

- Curriculum modification and planning for AG&T learners needs to scaffold and secure higher order learning objectives.

- School leadership needs to establish a coherent, 'joined-up' approach to assessment for learning and learning to learn through active research into the impact of current provision.

Effective classroom provision for AG&T

> **Effective provision for AG&T learners incorporates the following factors:**
>
> - A learning environment that expects and celebrates excellence
> - A differentiated, open-ended approach, enriched by both critical and creative thinking
> - It can be modelled and stimulated through appropriate textual frameworks or starting points
> - Learners are helped to perceive connections and appreciate links across diverse areas of study
> - A personalised understanding of learning needs and styles is promoted.

This chapter looks at provision for AG&T learners made through quality-first teaching in the classroom. While some of the examples provided are subject and/or age-specific, more typically the materials are generic and methodological in nature, aimed at stimulating adoption and adaptation to particular teaching contexts and subject areas. Again, the emphasis is on informing professional development opportunities for individual teachers, planning groups and whole-staff training programmes.

Overview of provision

Traditionally, provision for AG&T pupils drew upon one or more of the following elements.

Extra-curricular challenges

Some schools take the view that alongside effective classroom differentiation, the main body of AG&T provision comes through offering additional learning opportunities outside the mainstream curriculum. Such events may include:

- Saturday classes for a target year group or all/part of the AG&T cohort

- theme days (such as learning to learn days or creative challenge days)

- problem-solving and egg race competitions

- away weekends (e.g. at field study centres such as Flatford Mill)

- school visits to community resources supporting enhanced learning

- after-school masterclass programmes or interest groups

- summer school study weeks

- lunchtime/after-school clubs.

All such activities offer AG&T pupils the opportunity to develop their expertise alongside similar peers at a level of intensity difficult to emulate within the common curriculum. In addition to enhancing learning, associating with like-minded pupils helps able youngsters develop a positive self-image.

Extension

Developing extension resources and activities allows teachers to plan for continuity and progression in learning for their more able pupils. At its most basic, extension planning simply means having something to do beyond more of the same for the youngsters who finish or exhaust the core work early. Extension opportunities can be harder examples of the same activity, explore a topic in greater depth or breadth or simply be discrete activities in their own right intended to stimulate interest and/or widen understanding of a subject area. One benefit of extension work as a differentiating tool is that it helps prevent coasting or working to a standard level of expectation. At its best extension opportunities should provide a positive stimulus to all pupils to move through their basic skills work towards more advanced applications.

Pathways and group activities

Developing lessons on a common topic but providing various pathways (with varying degrees of challenge) through the material is another way of matching task to ability. An alternative solution is to differentiate *by task* within the class, giving different challenges to different ability groups or individuals according to assessed learning needs.

Enrichment activities

Enrichment activities attempt to improve the quality of pupil thinking. Structured programmes exist to promote this objective in both subject-specific and generic terms. More flexibly, teachers can simply incorporate cognitively challenging questioning systematically into their everyday teaching so as to develop higher level thinking skills. The Philosophy for Children (P4C) approach, for example, envisages a community of enquiry in which Socratic methods of questioning are used to extend independent thinking and concept development. Typically, it is the follow-up question(s) to an initial answer that generates the increased cerebral activity, as in:

- clarification questions ('do you mean ... ?', 'could you say that in another way?')

- justification questions ('why do you say that?', 'how do you know?', 'could you explain why?')

- concept questions ('is this always true?', 'what do you mean by?')

- consistency questions ('do you/does it agree with what was said before?')

Any effective enrichment approach addresses the needs of AG&T learners by promoting open-ended intellectual engagement and depth of thought, either within a given topic or as a means of developing intellectual horsepower that can be transferred to a range of learning contexts.

Open-ended questioning

Differentiation *by outcome* describes an activity intended for all of a class with the expectation that each individual will respond according to ability. For this to occur the tasks and questions posed need to be sufficiently open-ended to include and challenge pupils across the entire ability range. In mixed-ability settings this is not always easy. Established models of open-endedness do exist to assist teachers in framing such questions. For example, children thinking about their school and its environment could be asked to:

- speculate (e.g. 'what will schools be like in 10 years time?')

- reason (e.g. 'what subjects should be taught in school')

- discriminate (e.g. 'what makes for a good lesson?')

- problem-solve (e.g. 'how could the school become greener?')

The diversity of valid responses to such questions illustrates how open-endedness can give AG&T pupils the opportunity to experiment and develop their ideas freely.

Higher order thinking skills

Differentiation through open-endedness can be made more systematic still by drawing on the full range of higher order thinking processes. Itemisations of thinking skills can provide a useful template for teachers seeking to engage and develop pupils across all levels of thinking associated with a given topic. Typically a distinction is made between 'lower order' thinking (the acquisition and comprehension of knowledge) and the higher levels of thought associated with the application, analysis, synthesis (or creative use) and evaluation of that knowledge. The distinction is useful at the level of individual lesson planning as it allows teachers to assess whether the questions asked address all areas of thinking and not simply those centred around knowledge and understanding. It is also useful for wider curriculum planning in assessing whether activities are sufficiently varied to develop all levels of intellectual engagement with a given topic.

Creativity

Creativity in the classroom is open-ended in that it encourages pupils to produce something unique by drawing on individual skills, conceptual awareness and cultural context. The UK government-commissioned report, *All Our Futures: Creativity, Culture and Education* (DfEE, 1999), found that all learners can become more creative with practice. The definition of creativity used by the report was that creative thinking was always imaginative but also purposeful in terms of achieving its objective, which should be original and of value in relation to its objective.

Creative thinking also involves higher order thinking. It is linked to synthesis in that creative minds perceive connections and unities that are not immediately evident and can be surprising, delightful, apt and sometimes even original. It is also fundamental to application-type thinking, where prior knowledge is used to solve problems in an innovative or elegant manner. As Sternberg powerfully sets out in *Wisdom, Intelligence, and Creativity Synthesized* (2007), creative ability is key to most areas of high accomplishment in life. It is also an ability that can be developed through practice, encouragement and a clear focus on appropriate learning outcomes from teachers.

Accordingly, activities and questions may be planned systematically to exercise those qualities of mind that underpin creative endeavour. As the identification criteria for creative performance suggest, these include:

- *Fluency of thought and action*, which can be encouraged through the generation of multiple approaches, solutions or answers to problems and through questions requiring brainstorming for numerous answers such as 'how many things/words/ways/ideas/etc. can you think of to ... '

- *Flexibility and tenacity* of response to problem-solving via original, lateral or unconventional approaches which need the plasticity of mind that can be acquired through puzzles, Sudoku, tangrams, brain-teasers, conundrums, three-dimensional jigsaws, crosswords and similar aides to mental aerobics

- *Originality* or the production of new, quirky, unusual, non-stereotypical, 'out of the box' responses of a type that can be encouraged through questions which force the generation of unusual connections and ideas (such as 'how many uses can you think of for a spoon?') or consciously engineer the type of metaphorical thinking which underpins the creative imagination (e.g. 'how many ways is a leaf like a school?')

- *Elaboration* or the creative ability to add detail or complexity to a given stimulus – which may be a half-formed image, a group of randomly chosen articles, a newspaper cutting or picture or any other judiciously chosen (but skeletal or incomplete) artefact which the child may use to scaffold a more finished object or use to get to a more considered solution.

Exercising creative thinking skills trains pupils to generate ideas, pose questions and establish new ways of seeing. It helps them to go on to make practical use of the knowledge base they acquire in school. For this reason creative thinking is at the heart of providing for the able child. It is one of the twin pillars of higher mental functioning, often seen in tandem with critical thinking; the processes of logical and deductive reasoning aligned to thinking styles such as analysis and evaluation.

Extension planning: must … could … should

This planning model (Figure 5.1) is based on the text of *Goldilocks and the Three Bears* set out in the Appendix. The method is, of course, freely adaptable to a wide range of stimulus material/focus activities.

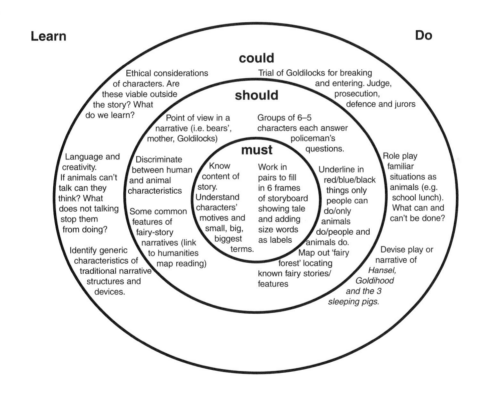

Figure 5.1 Extension planning linking learning objectives to activities

This model envisages a common classroom experience with key learning objectives ('learn' hemisphere) and corresponding activities ('do' hemisphere) for most pupils. The 'must' ring identifies the core learning/activity, while the 'should' envisages a progression route appropriate for most pupils. This layer draws on some higher order thinking skills (e.g. analysis, application and some synthesis). The 'could' layer takes the challenges of the 'should' activities and extends them into more complex and creative areas. Pupils may either move on to 'could' activities after completing 'should' or jump straight to 'could' for an appropriate level of challenge.

Higher order thinking and differential questioning

One method of securing open-endeness, differentiation of challenge and cognitive development across the breadth of thinking is to offer all pupils a hierarchical range of engagements within a given topic or text. Again, these model questions relate to the Goldilocks narrative set out in the Appendix.

Knowledge questions

The recall of specific information, terminology, technique or usage, for example:

- Who was Goldilocks?

- Where did she live?

- With whom?

- What did her mother tell her not to do?

- What did she do in the bear's house?

Comprehension questions

The understanding of what was read or said so it may be explained, for example:

- Why didn't her mother want her to go to the forest?

- What did Goldilocks look like?

- What kind of girl was she?

- Why did Goldilocks like the little bear's chair best?

Application questions

The converting of abstract content to concrete situations, problem-solving, for example:

- What do you think Goldilocks would have done if she'd come into your house?

- Write a sign that should be placed near the edge of the forest.

- Draw a picture/blueprint/aerial photograph showing what the bears' house looks like.

- Draw a map of the forest showing Goldilocks' house, the bears' house, etc.

- Turn the story into a play and act it out.

Analysis questions

The investigation/dissection of content to draw conclusions, for example:

- What parts of the story could not have actually happened? How do you know?

- In what ways do the bears act like humans?

- Do the bears behave like a real family? In what ways?

Synthesis questions

The connection and combination of ideas from within and outside the material, for example:

- How might the story have been different if it was Goldilocks and the three fishes?

- Write/tell/act the story of Goldihood and the Three Big Bad Beauties.

- Make a puppet out of one of the characters and act out his/her part in the story.

- Make a diorama of the bear's house and forest.

Evaluation questions

The judgement of worth, effectiveness, success, aesthetic merit value, motivation or morality, for example:

- Why were the bears angry with Goldilocks?

- Was Goldilocks a good girl or not? Why?

- What do you think she learned by going into that house?

- Why do you think the story of Goldilocks has been told to children for many years?

This model shows how even simple subject matter can stimulate advanced thinking skills. The question asking how the bears were like humans, for example, has challenged 5-year-olds to apply their understanding of the characteristics of human beings to the fairy tale form and has involved groups of secondary pupils in debate about the nuclear family, patriarchy, chauvinism, gender stereotypes and parenting. Similarly, the synthesis question inviting the construction of a narrative combining the elements of a variety of traditional tales provided a highly productive stimulus for a group of 30 exceptionally able 11-year-olds working in drama-based groups on a Saturday morning AG&T class. An example of pupils' critical and creative thinking on the differences between animals and humans in the narrative can be seen in Figure 5.2.

Actions and characteristics in *Goldilocks and the Three Bears*		
Human only	**Human and animal**	**Animal only**
In the bears' house there were three chairs ... there were also thee bowls ... upstairs there were three beds	The three bears lived in a house in the forest	He showed his long sharp claws and huge fangs
Mother bear made some porridge for breakfast	The porridge was too hot to eat	
Father bear said ...	Go for a walk in the forest	
She knocked at the door	She saw the bear's house and wanted to see who lived there ... she pushed open the door and went inside	
She tried a spoonful ...	She was hungry	
	She gobbled it all up	
	She sat on father bear's ... mother bear's ... baby bear's chair and it broke	
Upstairs	She was tired ... she lay on [the beds] and went to sleep	
	The three bears came back from their walk	Father bear roared
Someone's been eating my porridge mother bear added more calmly ... baby bear said tearfully	Tell that someone had been sitting in them	Showing his fierce teeth
	Father bear was furious	
Cleaned the bedroom ... made a new chair	The noise woke Goldilocks and she was frightened	

Figure 5.2

Critical thinking and creative thinking

Traditionally, the distinction between critical thinking and creative thinking was seen in terms of the right and left hemisphere functions of the brain – see Figure 5.3.

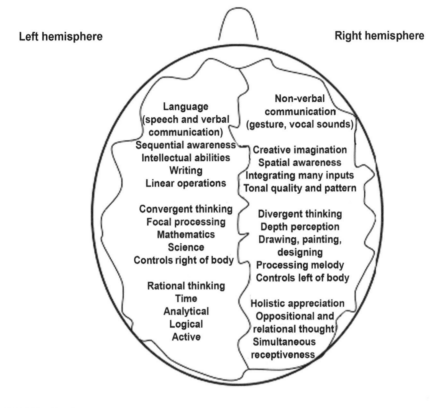

Left hemisphere

Language (speech and verbal communication)
Sequential awareness
Intellectual abilities
Writing
Linear operations

Convergent thinking
Focal processing
Mathematics
Science
Controls right of body

Rational thinking
Time
Analytical
Logical
Active

Right hemisphere

Non-verbal communication (gesture, vocal sounds)
Creative imagination
Spatial awareness
Integrating many inputs
Tonal quality and pattern

Divergent thinking
Depth perception
Drawing, painting, designing
Processing melody
Controls left of body

Holistic appreciation
Oppositional and relational thought
Simultaneous receptiveness

Figure 5.3 The brain

The left hemisphere was felt to deal with the deductive reasoning processes that lead to (converge on) logically correct solutions. By contrast, the right hemisphere was seen as processing divergent thoughts and the integration, synthesis and connection of many ideas together into holistic constructs. While this is a useful way of conceptualising the distinction between linear and non-linear thinking, the examples of critical and creative thinking activities just examined show that in practice both of these aspects of mental functioning are interrelated across both hemispheres in a much more complex process of neural interconnectivity and synchronicity than was hitherto recognised by many brain-centred educational formulations. Recent neuroscientific research (as summarised for educationalists, for example, by Professor John Geake (2009) in *The Brain at School*) has revealed how taxonomies of learning styles and left/right models of thinking can lead teachers into an excessive and unhelpful focus on dislocated strands of presumed mental functioning at the expense of more holistic challenges which activate a fuller range of learning and thinking styles.

The narrative synthesising *Hansel and Gretel*, *Goldilocks*, *Sleeping Beauty* and *The Three Little Pigs*, for example, is a creative activity that draws simultaneously on evaluative analyses of the features of the individual narratives to be combined. Similarly, the Goldilocks courtroom trial activity, requires an evaluative understanding of the behaviour of the characters before creating the drama in which the balance of right and wrong is established (see Figure 5.4).

Good and bad/right and wrong in *Goldilocks and the Three Bears*	
Thinking style	Evaluation (within a moral/behavioural context)
Learning objective(s)	To assess, appraise and compare behaviour of character within a narrative and to understand how improvement could be conceived
Method	In pairs underline words/phrases/incidents that show negative (bad) and positive (good) behaviour of characters. Use red and black for this. Draw up chart. _(chart below)_ NB: More able children can differentiate between father, mother and baby bear in a 4 column grid.
Development	1. Develop second grid (pairs into fours) which agrees three most serious mistakes made by Goldilocks in column one and in column two lists recommended alternatives (i.e. what she should have done) 2. Produce script for trial of G for breaking and entering, criminal damage and theft (4–8s – judge, defence, prosecution, Goldilocks, three bears, mother). NB: Show Terry Jones' *Wind in the Willows* trial scene as a model and provide appropriate legal vocabulary.
Further extension	3. Produce script (pairs into fours) and enact alternative play version in which G makes friends with the bears and stays for breakfast. Possible title – *Goldilocks Shows the Bears she Cares*.
Assessment and self-assessment criteria	The activities will reveal ability to: *assess, appraise, judge* actions; *compare/discuss* behaviour; *recommend* alternatives; *defend and/or justify* behaviour; *conclude* judgements; *trial* alternatives and *improve* outcomes.

Chart within Method:

Golidilocks		3 Bears	
Red (bad)	Black (good)	Red (bad)	Black (good)

Figure 5.4 Planning to combine critical and creative thinking objectives

Again the critical thinking provides the necessary understanding to embark on the creative construct, which depends on the quality of the critical analysis for its content (see Figure 5.5).

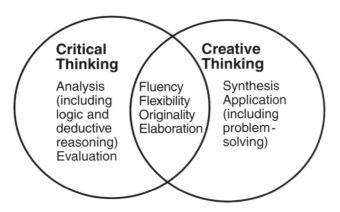

Figure 5.5 Critical and creative competencies

Clearly, such intrinsic links between critical and creative thinking can mean that in practical terms activities planned to promote any one aspect of higher order thinking can also support others. Figure 5.6 'Active thinking competencies' gives an illustration of how this might work in the classroom.

It can be seen that Figure 5.6 draws on Benjamin Bloom's original hierarchical taxonomy of thinking skills (from lower – knowledge and comprehension – to higher – analysis, application, synthesis and evaluation) to establish what might be termed subordinate modes of thinking (and associated classroom activity) set out under each major thinking style, or domain (Bloom, 1956). It is the clarity of understanding around these competencies and activities that then allows for greater precision. It is these competencies that then allow for greater precision in the assessment of the activities being attempted. As personalisation depends on teacher and pupil clarity about learning, this is key knowledge for teachers teaching AG&T pupils and for the pupils themselves.

Critical thinking has been defined in a variety of ways:

- The ability to analyse facts, generate and organise ideas, defend opinions, make comparisons, draw inferences, evaluate arguments and solve problems

- A way of reasoning that demands adequate support for one's beliefs and an unwillingness to be persuaded unless support is forthcoming

- Analytical thinking for the purpose of evaluating what is read

- A conscious and deliberate process which is used to interpret or evaluate information and experiences with a set of reflective attitudes and abilities that guide thoughtful beliefs and actions

- The intellectually disciplined process of actively and skilfully conceptualising, applying, analysing, synthesising, and/or evaluating information gathered from, or generated by, observation, experience, reflection, reasoning, or communication, as a guide to belief and action

- Reasonable reflective thinking focused on deciding what to believe or do.

Clearly, the definitions overlap but when viewed collectively also provide a broad understanding of the processes involved – where critical thinking differs from creative thinking and, importantly, how critical thinking processes can help inform the quality of creative thinking. In the active thinking competencies chart (Figure 5.6) the underlined target competencies within the evaluation box informed the Goldilocks trial activity in which discussions take place, assessments and comparisons are made and improvements identified and recommended.

One final point to make in this context, however, is that, wherever critical and creative competencies reside in the brain, research and practice alike have shown that so far as the psychometric testing of intelligence is concerned (e.g. IQ or abstract reasoning tests, etc.) very limited success has been shown by any intervention strategy developed so far to raise measured intelligence. Unfortunately, where 'left brain' intellectual functioning is concerned, the answer to the question 'can education make you more intelligent?' seems to be – no it can't. In terms of making someone a more effective learner, a more tenacious problem-solver and a more creative user of the knowledge and intelligence at his or her disposal, however; the answer to the question, 'can education make you more creative?' is that, given appropriate activities and ongoing challenge, it both can and does. In this sense – alongside other clear advantages in terms of variety and interest and motivation – it is clear that developing the creative, investigative, problem-solving muscle of all learners is the most productive means available of ensuring that youngsters make the most of their potential as learners.

Text and models of thought

As the example of Goldilocks illustrates, it is often productive to use a focus text as the stimulus for thinking and creativity. In Act 1 of the play *Waiting for Godot,* the master Pozzo orders his slave Lucky to think for the entertainment of his audience. The resulting monologue is a long inconsequential ramble using the language and rhythm of academic debate, but empty of purpose and meaning. Similarly, school teachers often hope their pupils will become effective thinkers without providing them with the raw material, the contextual information, to think with. Clearly, asking pupils to research an unknown topic is an acceptable means of encouraging independent learning skills. Where the aim is to facilitate higher order thinking, however, it is important to provide them with the information and conceptual understanding – the words, the structures, the contexts, the world of ideas (the tools) – they need to think with and within. This is most easily achieved by establishing discrete textual models that provide the managed space for pupils to inhabit intellectually.

The P4C movement recognises this truth and frequently uses specially written or selected texts to stimulate the type of thinking and support the type of questioning required. It is not, however, necessary to draw on purpose-built texts for this.

Active thinking competencies/verbs

Knowledge		Comprehension		Application		Analysis		Synthesis		Evaluation	
Know		**Understand**		**Apply**		**Analyse**		**Synthesise**		**Evaluate**	
Describe	Reproduce	Match	Interpret	Organise	Illustrate	Compare	Contrast	Connect	Create	Criticise	Judge
Recognise	Copy	Restate	Extend	Generalise	Demonstrate	Classify	Explain	Compose	Invent	Support	Relate
Memorise	Label	Paraphrase	Translate	Dramatise	Calculate	Point out	Order	Originate	Organise	Consider	Weigh
Identify	Tabulate	Rewrite	Compare	Prepare	Complete	Distinguish	Breakdown	Hypothesise	Generalise	Critique	Assess
Locate	Select	Exemplify	Contrast	Produce	Modify	Categorise	Correlate	Develop	Modify	Recommend	Choose
Recite	List	Express	Order	Choose	Experiment	Differentiate	Diagram	Design	Substitute	Summarise	Verify
Quote	Name	Illustrate	Group	Sketch	Relate	Subdivide	Discriminate	Combine	Formulate	Appraise	Decide
State	Define	Explain	Infer	Solve	Discover	Infer	Illustrate	Role play	Integrate	Compare	Rank
Match	Defend	Defend	Predict	Show	Enact	Survey	Outline	Construct	Rearrange	Discriminate	Test
Collect	Show	Distinguish		Paint	Construct	Select	Prioritise	Produce	Rewrite	Convince	Grade
Show	Tell/retell	Summarise		Classify	Develop	Separate		Plan	Adapt	Conclude	Defend
Record				Change	Transfer			Collaborate	Devise	Explain	Justify

Some associated types of performance area/activity (to link to verbs e.g. application – *dramatise* painting)

Knowledge		Comprehension		Application		Analysis		Synthesis		Evaluation	
Events	Websites	Recordings	Diagram	Map	List	Data set	Conclusions	Article	Alternative	Conclude	Assess
People	Software	Dialogue	Graph	Project	Project	Questions	Syllogisms	Invention	Experiment	Recommend	Advise
Recordings	Film/video	Photographs	Statement	Forecast	Drama	Answers	Reports	Report	Play	Value	Improve
Articles	Plays	Paintings	Model	Diagram	Painting	Arguments	Surveys	Rule set	Book	Trial	
Books	Poems	Images	Implication	Illustration	Sculpture	Persuasion	Graphs	Standards	Hypothesis	Survey	
Newspapers	Textbook	Drama	Cause	Extension		Word	Patterns	Game	Question	Standard	
Magazines	Texts	Cartoon	Metaphor	Solution		choice	Parts	Song	Prediction	Compare	
Television		Story	Outline	Question		Statements		Machine		Discuss	

Figure 5.6 Active thinking competencies

Any object or artefact that is capable of revealing meaning or cultural significance may be defined as a text for the purposes of providing a scaffold for structured thought.

Examples of this are shown in the following activity.

Activity

The following questions and activities are drawn from the list of active thinking competencies. The aim is to simulate a way of promoting higher order thinking by drawing on a focus text. While working through the questions (as an independent exercise or in pairs/groups) consider how the text helps to support and structure the thinking.

Bishop: I'm afraid you've got a bad egg, Mr Jones
Nervous curate: Oh no, My Lord. I assure you! Parts of it are excellent!

Figure 5.7 *True Humility*
http://commons.wikimedia.org/wiki/File:True_humility.png

True Humility

This famous cartoon (Figure 5.7) was originally published in *Punch* magazine in 1895.

* Describe the scene shown in no more than 50 words.

* Why do you think the cartoon was called *True Humility*?

* Add thought bubbles to show what the bishop, the curate, one of the ladies at the table and the servant in the background are thinking at this moment.

* Draw a cartoon or develop a waxworks (*tableau vivant*) of a modern-day moment called *True Humility*. If one or more of the cartoon characters or waxwork models were brought to life what would they say?

* 'A curate's egg' is a phrase that came to mean good in parts. Make a list of at least 10 things that can be part good and part bad. What kind of things are they? Are there any things that cannot be part good and part bad but which once any part is bad must be all bad? What kind of things are these?

- Should the curate have told the truth? Think of a time when you have not told the whole truth to avoid getting into trouble or to spare someone's feelings. Is it possible that being economical with the truth can be a good thing or is it always better to be completely honest? What would have happened if you had told the full truth?

Now decide how you might use the following text to stimulate thinking and creativity.

Gluttony by Pieter Brueghel the elder

Figure 5.8 *Gluttony* **by Pieter Brueghel the elder**
with kind permission from the Israel Museum, Jerusalem

While there is no preferred solution for this activity, the following P4C questions might usefully be considered in association with the text (Figure 5.8) and may be freely adapted to fit other visual texts:

- What is happening in this picture? Why?

- Do the various goings on reveal anything in common? In what way?

- Are all the figures in the picture human? Why not?

- Are the non-human figures all animals? What are they doing? What do they represent?

- What title would you give the picture? Choose three characters and give them speech and/or thought bubbles.

- Can you think of any narrative that explains everything that is going on?

- Are there any lessons we can learn from this picture? What are they?

Developing creativity in the classroom: some practical ideas

The following additional strategies are useful ways of supporting creative learning in the classroom.

SCAMPER

This acronym brings together a number of the approaches outlined earlier as key to the creative elements of fluency, flexibility, originality and elaboration. SCAMPER may be applied in whole or part to any focus text or area of study as a means of generating right brain engagement with the subject matter in question.

S is for substitute. This may mean, for example, the substitution of another person into a narrative or a specific historical, cultural or social situation. It may also mean the substitution of another time or place or item into any given context. It might equally imply the substitution of another method or material or formula into one that was previously fixed. For example:

- How would Little Red Riding Hood have acted if she were in Goldilocks' shoes? How would baby bear have told the story?

- Write the scene in which Lady Macbeth goes to buy gloves in Topshop.

- What would an ancient Egyptian boy think if he time travelled to London for a week in 1850? Write his diary and/or his postcard back home.

- What if gold was as common as iron and iron as rare as gold?

C is for combine. Combinations may be of ideas or characters or objects. They may synthesise elements to create a new whole or they may juxtapose diverse items for a variety of effects. Combining products can make cooking creative. Seeing one object in terms of another is at the heart of figurative thinking (simile, metaphor, symbolism, etc.). Such activities include:

- Devising a narrative or a news report or a work of art or a formula in which a number of disparate objects or ideas are combined into a coherent product.

- Taking two or more objects (or books or organisms or number patterns) and identifying as many similarities and differences as possible.

- Having two separate lists or collections or items or materials and identifying as many points of connection between the two as possible.

- Turning words into pictograms; graphical symbols or pictorial representations of themselves (e.g. the word 'zoom' drawn as a rocket).

A is for adapt. Adaptation is about modifying or reapplying one thing so that it may be improved or used for another purpose. Questions such as 'how many uses can you think of for a tea towel?' or 'what improvements could you make to a vacuum cleaner or a favourite toy?' fit into this category. Others include:

- Developing an idea or rule or practice or way of working to address, solve or extend thinking about a seemingly unrelated problem. For example, 'what can we learn from a frog about the development of an amphibious car?'

- Using a technique common in one discipline to illuminate another (e.g. using a graph to map out fluctuations in a character's happiness or a flow chart to show options, choices and chain of causality impacting on a historical event).

- Adapting something from one genre to another (e.g. science experiment to poetry, 3rd person history to autobiography, a historical document to modern journalism, etc.).

M is for modify. Modification often involves making changes to suit particular objectives. For example, 'how could a teapot be made more amusing?' or 'what would we need to change to give *Of Mice and Men* a happy ending?' or 'how could the school car park be altered to make better use of the space?'

P is for put to use. At a basic level creative thinking of this type encompasses the type of divergent reasoning that asks 'how many uses can you think of for … a paper cup; the inside of a toilet roll; a frying pan; etc.'. In a more focused teaching context it may also lead towards a creative or ingenious solution to a particular problem or issue, as in 'how can the school's waste paper be used to save energy?' or 'how can a drop of oil, a gallon of water and a ruler help us work out the diameter of an atom?'

E is for eliminate. Examples of the creative use of elimination include:

- Extreme summary; everything from a one-sentence *Goldilocks* to a three-minute *King Lear*.

- 'Found' poetry or prose in which a piece of text is used as the basis for another writing to emerge. This may come through cutting out chunks of text and highlighting others to reveal another meaning hidden within the original.

- Developing overarching titles, paragraph headings, illustrations, captions and graphical representations (such as concept maps or matrices) as a way of capturing the essence of an informative text in an alternative way.

R is for rearrange. This could involve the making of a pattern from basic constituents, the construction of a larger picture or image from smaller fragments or shapes (as, e.g., in the traditional Chinese tangram puzzle) or the rearrangement of pieces to form a cube in a three-dimensional jigsaw. Rearrangement in the pursuit of meaning is a key factor in such activities as when pupils are asked to:

- Cut out headlines from a newspaper or magazine and recombine – cut and paste – them (along with any pictures or graphics) to produce a new narrative or text.

- Reconstruct or create a new artefact from a larger text – written, visual or three-dimensional – which has been cut up or deconstructed in some way to form the basis of a new entity.

Heterodox objects

John Donne's poem 'A Valediction Forbidding Mourning' compares the union between himself and his lover as like that between 'stiff twin compasses'. Later, the critic Dr Johnson coined the term metaphysical to describe such poems in which 'heterodox objects [are] yoked by violence together'.

Johnson's point was an aesthetic one. He found figures of speech that connected such disparate items as love and mathematics displeasing. The idea, however, that metaphorical thinking (or the capacity to see the significance of one thing through the characteristics of another) can be generated through seemingly arbitrary connections and combinations is a useful one in helping to develop the capacity for creative connection.

The English language is full of metaphor at every level. Highlighting productive, pleasing or surprising connections between 'heterodox' items is central to creativity and creative meaning-making. Activities designed to enrich the capacity to make connections and draw out the metaphorical fecundity of shared experience are an important means of developing the creative capacities of AG&T pupils.

The activities described below suggest a range of ways in which the capacity to yoke heterodox objects can be developed. As always, the generic methods described should be adapted to specific teaching contexts.

Similes and synthesis

Here the objective is to connect either adjectives to nouns (e.g. as *hungry* as a *wolf*) or to connect abstract nouns to concrete nouns (e.g. *virtue* is like *gold*). There are a number of ways of generating such connections depending on the number of variables and/or the degree of difficulty required. Examples include:

- Presenting two lists of words (say eight or 10 in each) with the challenge for pupils to come up with similes that they can justify and explain. This opens up the possibility of either offering relatively conventional connections – say: *busy, brave, deaf, hairy, mad, slippery, sly* and *tough* to connect with *eel, gorilla, beaver, fox, lion, post, hornet* and *boots* – or generating more imaginative conceptual links – say: *dry, easy, fast, obstinate, pretty, proud* and *silly* to connect with *lemon, badger, lead, day, saucepan, prune, money* and *pancake*. This approach also allows for even more creative applications in which pupils are given only one half of the simile (… *as* [something] *as a turtle; as bubbly as* …). Explaining the simile afterwards is key to the activity.

- Allowing for randomly generated similes. Here pupils are given access to two lists. In this example there are 10 words in each list; one list containing abstract words the other containing concrete words.

1. Power	1. Orange
2. Insult	2. Can of paint
3. Creativity	3. Crayon
4. Bravery	4. Sausage
5. Frustration	5. River
6. Potential	6. Pillow
7. Desire	7. Mountain
8. Trust	8. Oven
9. Praise	9. Husband
10. Impatience	10. Football

Using dice or cards, or any other method of obtaining random numbers, pupil pairings identify a word off each list. If numbers 2 then 4 come up, the pairs would then need to think of as many ways as they can in which an insult can be said to be like a sausage. (NB: Running an internet search for 'simile generator' will reveal a number of applications for generating similes automatically.)

- Allow for more considered connections by providing a number of alternatives to be selected according to perceived appropriateness. Have a simile box containing a variety of objects or images of objects. Depending on the level and nature of the required challenge these items could be selected as being resonant or evocative of particular moods or certain ways of seeing. For example, a dried leaf, an old house brick, a worn shoe, a pebble, an egg, a brush, a mirror, a used bus ticket, etc., etc. The task is to decide on the most appropriate object to use to illuminate a comparison with a second element in the simile. This corresponding half of the simile can be introduced in a number of ways depending on context. Such words may be randomly generated (e.g. through a second box of 'lucky-dip' words – for instance, beauty, revenge, education); or specifically introduced as part of work on a theme or topic (e.g. school, winter, history, war). Once the most appropriate object is decided upon, the task is then to brainstorm as many ways as possible in which the object chosen from the box could be said to be like the given word or concept. For example:

An *old house brick* is like *history* because:

- It was made in the past

- History is made of many connected events like a brick in a wall

- Each brick is like a day, part of a long wall from past to future

- Once something has happened it can't be changed, like a brick in mortar

- Bricks are made by humans and so is history

- Some things from history are ruined, like a broken-down house, etc.

Metaphor

A productive way of combining critical thinking with creative thinking is to ask pupils to match metaphorical meanings to more literal formulations of the same idea. Common sayings are a useful source of metaphor and there are many interactive ways in which pupils may be asked to connect similes and metaphors to their meanings.

Sayings	Meanings
A leopard cannot change its spots	Progress is rarely without difficulty
As you sow, so shall you reap	Children are like their parents
A rolling stone gathers no moss	You must accept the consequences of your actions
Every path has its puddle	If you are nice to me, I'll be nice to you
Fine words butter no parsnips	Get the basics right first
The apple doesn't fall far from the tree	Rumours usually have some truth in them
You scratch my back and I'll scratch yours	No amount of talking can replace action
The road to hell is paved with good intentions	A bad or unpleasant person can't become good or pleasant
Learn to walk before you run	If you intend to do something then do it
There's no smoke without fire	Someone who moves a lot has no friends, possessions or ties

Figure 5.9

See Figure 5.9 – here the task is to match saying to meaning. An extension to this activity when the initial connections have been made is to add a third column in which pupils develop a second saying with the same meaning. For example: You scratch my back and I'll scratch yours//If you are nice to me I'll be nice to you//Share your crisps and I'll give you some peanuts. Other approaches could include:

- Giving half the class/group a different metaphor or saying (on paper or to remember) and the other half literal meanings of the same expressions. The task is to find your match

- Distributing a range of metaphorical expressions and ask pupils to create a drawing or cartoon to illustrate, label, explain and entitle the image

- Break the metaphor in half (or for longer formulations/greater challenge, several pieces) and ask pupils to connect the pieces and justify their choice.

Scaffolding creative thinking

A useful scaffold for supporting the creative ability to establish connections and perceive links between heterodox objects is a mix-matrix. The approach is also effective for developing deductive reasoning skills. The basic technique is to present information in four bocks of three (12 cells) or four blocks of four (16 cells). The objective is to identify each subset of four from the mixed set. Using the example in Figure 5.10, in pairs decide on the four most likely groupings.

	A	B	C	D
1	Birds of a feather flock together	The road to hell is paved with good intentions	The apple doesn't fall far from the tree	No man is an island
2	Give someone enough rope and they'll hang themselves	If you chase two rabbits you'll not catch either one	As you sow, so shall you reap	Learn to walk before you can run
3	No smoke without fire	Still waters run deep	A bird in hand is worth two in the bush	Blood is thicker than water
4	Don't count your chickens before they're hatched	He who plays with fire gets burnt	Dogs of the same street bark alike	The pen is mightier than the sword

Figure 5.10

The groups originally intended were:

- A1, C1, C4 and D3 (the bonds of friendship and family)

- A4, B2, C3 and D2 (caution against unwarranted optimism or overreaching)

- A2, B1, B4 and C2 (the consequences/potential for self-damage of actions)

- A3, B3, D1 and D4 (wise maxim or aphorism expressing a general truth).

Using a mix-matrix as a vehicle for encouraging deductively robust reasoning skills to make sustainable analytical links across a subject or topic is certainly a valuable effect of this approach. In every curriculum area, a mix-matrix may be used to encourage non-linear understanding and joined-up thinking. In mathematics, for example, the jumbled solutions to four different problems, or else the various components of four algorithms, or perhaps four mathematical patterns could be provided for disentangling and uniting in meaning.

The potential of a mix-matrix approach, however, extends further than this. Pairs undertaking the mixed metaphor matrix may well have identified groups of four that differ from those suggested. Moreover the rationale behind these alternative groupings may be equally plausible and possibly more inventive than the 'official' answer on offer. Making connections can be more than a left-hemisphere exercise in deductive and inferential reasoning. Even in the most logically defensible set of fragments it is possible for more intuitive organising principles to be imagined. For example, a grouping of proverbs A4, B2, C2 and D2 might be argued on the basis of speaking directly to a second person addressee – you chase, you run, your chickens, you sow and reap.

The potential for heuristic learning – that is of establishing a context in which cerebral free-play and creativity are to the fore – is key to this approach. Where a teacher seeks to use a mix-matrix to sharpen up pupils' awareness of connections across topic boundaries, for example, the method may be as focused on accuracy as necessary. The approach, though, will always tend to generate unexpected connections and surprising new unities. Where this potential is recognised and celebrated a mix-matrix approach also provides the opportunity for deliberately exercising the pupils' capacity for establishing new unities and creating unexpected connections.

Clearly, this approach is a flexible one capable of being freely adapted to suit all ages and many learning objectives. For example:

- Using objects instead of a written matrix

- Providing a matrix with a number of blanks or elisions so that pupils need to decide on groupings and then on how they might be completed

- Focusing not so much on correct solutions as on coherent explanations of perceived groupings.

However the method is adapted, emphasis should always be placed on allowing pupils to justify their groupings and giving credit for the insight shown in so doing.

 Activity

In pairs or small groups agree on four subsets for the mix-matrix given in Figure 5.11. Is it possible also to identify a single connecting theme or unifying element? It is important for each pair/group to be as precise as possible in defining the connecting criteria for each subset and any overarching commonality that might be identified. Twenty to thirty minutes should be allowed for this part of the activity. Where possible pairs/groups should then share their conclusions with other participants. Questions for this plenary session include:

	A	B	C	D
1	**STENCIL**	American Typewriter	**Playbill**	Plantagonet Cherokee
2	*Mistral*	Ζαπφ Δινγβατσ	DESDEMONA	▶📦🚲♥ⓘ●■?
3	**Marker Felt**	PERPETUA TITLING MT	Chalkboard	Lucida Bright
4	Gill Sans	Μονοτυπε Σορτσ	Papyrus	✢⽊■℔⏧⽊■℔✦

Figure 5.11

- Is it possible to arrive at a consensus or do opinions vary too markedly to agree on one single solution?

- Do some solutions appear qualitatively superior to others or do they all seem equally plausible?

- What does it feel like to be involved in so open-ended an activity? What type of learning ensued?

- How might such an approach be used to provide challenge across the curriculum in specific subject areas?

In fact the 16 cells all contain not only the name but the form of an electronic font. So Chalkboard is written as Chalkboard and Wingdings as ✦⽊■℔⏧⽊■℔✦ etc. The original selection criteria were:

- four fonts using symbols to represent letters

- four fonts suggesting female names

- four fonts relating to writing and stationery equipment

- four fonts with names starting with the letter P

Because of some deliberate overlaps and ambiguities (such as Perpetua Titling MT starting with a P and also sounding like a female name) it is probable that many solutions to the activity draw on different connecting principles. The expectation is that the creative challenge, collaborative thinking and heuristic reasoning involved in coming up with an appropriate response to the mix-matrix justifies the approach.

One virtue of the mix-matrix, however, is that it supports a wide variety of challenge and follow-up activity. Adaptations to the basic method include:

- Differentiation of the level of openness and/or the number of variables within the basic matrix (e.g. pupils may be asked for pairs rather than fours and have eight or 12 rather than 16 variables)

- A greater or lesser degree of logical/deductive connection, encouraging either high level analytical processes, or (where fewer rational links obtain) a high level synthesis of more heterodox or more intuitively linked materials

- A more diverse mixture of media, including perhaps words, artefacts, images, sounds and even tastes to distinguish between and connect.

Follow-up activities may draw on the solutions to the mix-matrix to scaffold and support further creative work. For example, pupils working on the mixed font matrix might be told that the 16 elements of the matrix combine to make up the detail of a short story entitled *The School Play* and that there are four groups of four which provide paragraph information for each of four paragraphs to be used for the body of the story. Alternatively, pupils might be told that these are the 16 clues to a crime and their task is to solve the mystery.

Scaffolding independent learning

The mix-matrix model is a useful example of how a teaching method may either seek to secure correct responses to a problem by encouraging the processes of deductive reasoning or else provide a structure within which more creative connections are supported and fostered. For AG&T learners, it is important to provide structured opportunities for youngsters to develop confidence as independent learners and – within the context of personalisation – to have the opportunity to develop their own learning agendas. For this process to become embedded in classroom practice, however, teaching needs actively to scaffold and model opportunities for independence. The following case study raises a number of questions and points towards a number of solutions about how this may be achieved within the context of whole-class teaching.

Case study

The following extract is the opening to a short story written by the author as part of a series of narratives supporting independent higher order thinking. While the characters are fictitious, the opinions and events (as well as the narrator's perceived connection between *Macbeth* and her school and local area) are an accurate rendition of a genuine occurrence.

Thunder and lightning. Enter three witches

First Witch: When shall we three meet again?

In thunder, lightning, or in rain?

Second Witch:	When the hurly-burly's done,
	When the battle's lost and won.
Third Witch:	That will be ere the set of sun.
First Witch:	Where the place?
Second Witch:	Upon the heath.
Third Witch:	There to meet with Macbeth.
First Witch:	I come, Grimalkin.
Second Witch:	Paddock calls.
Third Witch:	Anon.
All Witches:	Fair is foul, and foul is fair,
	Hover through the fog and filthy air.

Florence Ann Banks stared contemptuously at the book and piece of paper on the desk in front of her. Life, she thought, and not for the first time, was just not *fair*. She couldn't even see what was wrong with the comment she'd made. She certainly couldn't see why she was now losing her break time because of it. Neither could the rest of 5M she thought. Everyone had laughed like drains when she'd said it. She smiled at the memory of the sudden injection of humour into Mr Duncan's English lesson. Goodness knows it had needed it she thought. It wasn't exactly boring she considered, that wouldn't be fair. It was quite interesting in fact, but it was all so serious, so … what was that word her father used: *dire*, no not dire, *dour*, that was it DOUR. Mr Duncan was so strict, such a stickler for good behaviour in class that everyone was on a knife edge, trying to be well-behaved but always struggling to keep what he called 'inappropriate behaviour' beneath the surface. Sometimes something had to give, like her granny's pressure cooker when she'd left it on the gas too long, letting off a head of steam.

'What was that remark Florence?' Duncan had asked when she'd unwisely whispered it to bigmouth Freddie Siward, her talk partner for the starter activity in that morning's lesson. Siward, of course, had deliberately landed her in it by letting out an exaggerated snorting guffaw, drawing everyone's attention to them both.

'Nothing sir', she'd fibbed, hoping he'd just let it pass by telling them to get on with their work, as teachers often do once they'd demonstrated to everyone else in the class that they were vigilant for any slight lapse in behaviour. But not this time, he was looking to make some sort of point she thought.

'Come along, it couldn't have been nothing. Let's all hear what's so amusing about the three witches. I enjoy a good joke.'

Florence knew this to be a lie 10 times more foul than her own untruth, knew for certain, in fact, that there was nothing Duncan enjoyed less than a good laugh. She decided though that this time she wouldn't be cowed by his sarcasm. Actually, she thought what she'd said was worth sharing.

(Continued)

(Continued)

'I said they're like Miss Ross, Miss Lennox and Miss Menteith, Sir.'

At this the more perceptive in the class began to giggle but were immediately silenced by Duncan's upheld palm, raised to head height in what Florence thought was the manner of a policeman calming traffic. He continued in pursuit of his quarry: her.

'Who are like Ms Ross, Lennox and Menteith?' he persisted, knowing full well who.

'The three witches sir,'

'Oh, I see, so pray enlighten us. In what way do you think the head and deputies of this school resemble the three witches in Shakespeare's Macbeth?'

He was setting himself up, Florence could tell, to make fun of whatever reason she came up with, to make her sound silly, pathetic. That was how he worked. She'd seen him do it before. Only this time, she knew she had something that was actually quite smart. Disrespectful, yes; unkind, perhaps; untrue, certainly – but undoubtedly smart. So she let him have it.

'It's like them planning to meet their boyfriends in the pub on the heath after school sir.'

It was at that point that the pressure cooker popped and everyone in the class rocked with laughter, seeing in their mind's eye, Florence hoped, their three most important teachers dressed as witches, with black teeth and hairy chins, possibly on broomsticks, going out onto the heath at the end of the day to meet these strange-sounding individuals Grimalkin, Paddock and Macbeth for a glass of hemlock and a crafty cuddle in the Hare and Billet. That was certainly the image she had in her mind.

Inevitably, Duncan had to regain control and the way he did it – predictable though effective – was to ask her to remain behind at break time to discuss the matter further and to invite anyone else who wanted to join her to continue laughing.

Clearly, what we see here is a teacher – no doubt eager to proceed with his own planned activities and sustain his control over a lively class – fail (at least in Florence's eyes) to rise to the challenge of the unanticipated observation connecting the witches with members of staff. However understandable Mr Duncan's response might appear within the context of classroom management, the question to ask is how might he have responded to Florence's insight in such a way as to allow her personal response to the focus text to inform and encourage her individual engagement with a challenging new text.

Consider the following possibilities:

- Encouraging Florence to extend her sense of contemporary connection by producing a school-based version of the witches incantation to be read to the class in contrast to the Shakespearean original

- Suggesting that as the reading continues Florence and the rest of the class make notes about any other possible contemporary analogies to the events/

dialogue in the play and for these to be pooled later in a student-led updating of the drama set in and around the school

- Praise Florence for her insight, request that for the moment she continues reading with the class while developing her idea and at break time, rather than punishing her, give her a recorder and script and propose that she approaches the members of staff concerned and ask them to provide a reading of the lines for Florence to introduce at the start of the next lesson.

Further questions to discuss in response to this case study include:

- What would be the advantages and disadvantages of any/all of these responses?

- How else might Mr Duncan have supported rather than squashed Florence's independent thinking?

- From a teaching perspective, what would you say are the advantages and risks of allowing student-led thinking to shape classroom learning in the manner suggested?

- What differences in planning and classroom management are required to allow independent and/or student-led learning to flourish?

Cross-reference

One issue previously touched on in relation to independent learning is the linearity of curriculum delivery itself. The discussion around cross-curricular/ creative curriculum planning in Chapter 4 established the current interest in supporting student learning by actively connecting several strands of subject-specific learning objectives into overarching topic- or theme-based units more effectively to support joined-up thinking and learning. While it is the role of leadership to provide and promote the developmental opportunities to make this objective achievable for classroom teachers, it is nevertheless the teachers themselves, either individually or in year group planning teams, who will construct the short- and medium-term plans that will secure the necessary schemes of work in support of non-linear learning models. The challenge of such an approach is to ensure that the units of work so developed also provide an appropriate level of challenge alongside opportunities for creative, independent, student-led learning. The concluding activity of this chapter sets out a model for such a planning objective (that may be freely adapted by substituting setting-specific learning objectives to replace the examples provided).

 ## Activity

This simulated planning model draws once again on an image from Brueghel, this time his 1565 painting *Hunters in the Snow*, which can be found on Wikipedia.

(Continued)

(Continued)

The areas of learning which the topic intends to cover are as follows:

Geography

Pupils should learn to:

- Ask geographical questions – e.g. 'What is this landscape like?'

- Analyse evidence and draw conclusions

- Use atlases, globes, maps and plans at a range of scales (e.g. use contents, keys, grids)

- Use secondary sources of information (e.g. texts, internet, images, pictures)

- Use ICT to help in geographical investigations

- Identify and describe what places are like (e.g. weather, jobs, etc.)

- Describe where places are (e.g. town, countryside, rivers, mountains, etc.)

- Explain why places are like they are

- Identify how and why places differ and change.

Science

Pupils should learn to:

- Think creatively to explain how things work and establish links between cause and effect

- Consider what sources of information they will use to answer questions

- Use a wide range of methods, including diagrams, drawings, tables, bar charts, line graphs and ICT, to communicate data in an appropriate and systematic manner

- Make comparisons and identify simple patterns or associations in their own observations and measurements or other data

- Use observations, measurements or other data to draw conclusions.

Art & design

Pupils should learn to:

- Compare ideas, methods and approaches in their own and others' work and say what they think and feel about them

- Adapt their work according to their views and describe how they might develop it further

- Appreciate materials and processes used in art, craft and design and how these can be matched to ideas and intentions

- Understand the roles and purposes of artists, craftspeople and designers working in different times and cultures (for example, Western Europe and the wider world)

- Explore a range of starting points for practical work (e.g. images, stories, music, natural and made objects and environments)

- Work on their own, and collaborate with others, on projects in two and three dimensions

- Use a range of materials and processes, including ICT (e.g. painting, collage, print making, digital media, textiles, sculpture)

- Investigate art, craft and design in a variety of genres, styles and traditions.

History

Pupils should learn to:

- Identify characteristic features of the periods and societies studied, including the ideas, beliefs, attitudes and experiences of men, women and children in the past

- Describe and make links between the main events, situations and changes within and across the different periods and societies studied

- Find out about the events, people and changes studied from an appropriate range of sources of information, including ICT-based sources (e.g. documents, CD-ROMS, databases, pictures, music, artefacts, historic buildings, museums, sites, etc.).

Music

Pupils should learn to:

- Improvise, developing rhythmic and melodic material when performing

(Continued)

(Continued)

- Explore, choose, combine and organise musical ideas within musical structures

- Use the musical elements of pitch, duration, dynamics, tempo, timbre, texture and silence to communicate different moods and effects

- Produce music in different ways (e.g. through the use of different resources, such as ICT)

- Appreciate a range of live and recorded music from different times and cultures.

ICT

Pupils should learn to:

- Develop and refine ideas by bringing together, organising and reorganising text, tables, images and sound as appropriate (e.g. desktop publishing, multimedia presentations)

- Share and exchange information in a variety of forms, including email (e.g. displays, posters, animations, musical compositions)

- Work with others to explore a variety of information sources and ICT tools (e.g. searching the internet for information about a different part of the world, designing textile patterns using graphics software, using ICT tools to capture and change sounds).

The aim is to examine the topic stimulus alongside the range of potential learning intentions to develop a half-term (six-week) programme of activities that provide a coherent learning platform for pupils of all abilities. The objective is not necessarily to cover all of the learning criteria for all six subjects (though this may be achievable). It is rather to establish a cross-curricular range of connected learning activities to challenge all pupils including the most able. This may be achieved through a variety of open-ended activities suitable for all learners or through a core programme of common activities augmented by enrichment, extension and independent learning opportunities as appropriate. It is anticipated that approaches supporting critical and creative thinking identified throughout this chapter will assist in completing this planning activity. The chart setting out active thinking competencies and activities, for example, should assist in generating a broad spectrum of activity in response to the thematic starting point(s) in Brueghel's painting. As an exercise in group planning this activity could take up to one hour.

Supporting and evaluating the planning activity

When taking feedback on this activity, the aim is not to distinguish acceptable from less acceptable responses. Rather, the purpose is to simulate a medium-term planning process in which the learning needs of AG&T pupils are given equal consideration to those of middle and lower ability learners. To offer a range of activities for comparison with those generated in professional development groups, however, the following suggestions may provide a basis for further evaluation:

- A focus on weather via the production of four seasonal triptychs or installations – summer, autumn, winter, spring. The main panel on each triptych to display a local scene revealing the appointed season with the two smaller panels illustrating aspects of the same season, one from the perspective of a historical period (say Victorian), the other showing characteristic seasonal activities from another country or region (say North Eastern China). Pupils work individually, in pairs and groups using ICT and reference material to research each aspect of their season and:

    (i) Produce and illustrate data relating to the focus of each panel showing trends in climate, comparative information, production statistics, cause and effect relationships, changes over time and across regions, characteristic geographical features associated with the climate/season, etc.

    (ii) Use a variety of appropriate techniques and multimedia approaches to reveal seasonal variations – collage, montage/photo-montage, textiles, digital images, artefacts, three-dimensional objects, etc.

    (iii) Make representations of the seasons, time-periods and geographical locations drawing on different artistic styles (e.g. representational in the manner of Brueghel, impressionistic in the manner of Van Gogh's landscapes, abstract in the style of Picasso's Mediterranean landscapes and formulaic in the manner of traditional Chinese landscape painting) with the paintings to reveal seasonally appropriate landscape.

- Making music to accompany each display – using ICT and other devices – with the aim of encapsulating the mood of the particular season. Compare this with music produced in the historical period and/or region being studied. What differences are there to be noted? What improvements/modifications need to be made.

- Prepare a PowerPoint or other multimedia presentation (music, moving images) with a prepared talk to illustrate information about a focus season as it was seen historically, as it is experienced in a different culture and in the present day locally. Emphasis should be placed on similarities and differences across time and around the world.

- Use the first verse of Christina Rosetti's poem, 'In the Bleak Midwinter', to reveal winter similes and metaphor (In the bleak midwinter,//frosty wind made moan,// Earth stood hard as iron,//water like a stone). Clearly other appropriate winter poems may be substituted as necessary. The task is to generate/research as many seasonally descriptive words – such as *bleak* for winter – as possible.

The development is to use the most productive of these to generate seasonal similes to form part of each display – incorporating pictograms and other illustration techniques to draw out the meaning of the image.

- Devise a range of mix-matrix challenges inviting connections between the four seasons in their differing geographical, climactic and historical contexts.

- Take 4 seasonal paintings and generate/tabulate lists of similarities and differences. A development from this is to look at 'Crabbed Age and Youth' – possibly composed by Shakespeare in 1599:

> CRABBÈD Age and Youth
> Cannot live together:
> Youth is full of pleasance,
> Age is full of care;
> Youth like summer morn,
> Age like winter weather;
> Youth like summer brave,
> Age like winter bare.
> Youth is full of sport,
> Age's breath is short;
> Youth is nimble, Age is lame;
> Youth is hot and bold,
> Age is weak and cold.

Use this to support in drawing or making three-dimensional models of the seasons personified as individually appropriate characters.

- Analyse board games such as Monopoly and Cluedo. Identify 10 key characteristics. Groups then given two dice, two decks of plain cards and a square of board. The challenge is to produce a board game called Seasons in which the information gained through the project about the four seasons, including their positive and negative aspects, help or hinder players towards a winning position on New Year's Eve.

- Groups develop their own waxwork or *tableaux vivant* to represent their season. The frozen image should have a title and individuals produce thought and/or speech bubbles to reveal their thinking.

- Use the internet to research/gather information/images about winter weather in North Europe during the sixteenth century (Brueghel and Shakespeare's time), the Victorian and the modern period. What are the differences/trends and how can they best be illustrated? What has caused the changes? What other effects have these changes had? What will happen if they continue? A task is to draw up a chart with four columns – Cause, Effect, Consequence for Future and Advice for Action.

Clearly, the key to evaluating such joined-up planning activities is to determine whether the programme offers a sufficient degree of challenge and flexibility for all learners including the more able. By design, relatively little attention has been given in this chapter to the type of provision that is differentiated for able learners through access to more difficult or complex work. This is not because challenge of this sort is not appropriate but because this material is readily available and familiar to most teachers. As we anticipate the next chapter that discusses parental support for learning, however, it is worth noting that the type of challenge represented by difficult content is both important where it meets learning need AND it is the aspect of provision that is most familiar to most parents. While there is no sense of either/or in discussions of the efficacy of difficult work or creative challenge (both of course being necessary) it is important to ensure that parents are informed and supportive of all approaches taken by schools to support their youngsters. The next chapter examines ways in which this might be achieved.

To think about

- What aspects of the provision outlined in this chapter do you feel to be most useful for incorporating into your own classroom practice?

- What support from the setting do you feel you would like to help you improve provision for your AG&T learners?

- Do you know how to set about obtaining the support you need to take the next steps in this area of development?

Summary

A number of key points have been made in this chapter regarding classroom planning and provision.

- There are a generic range of approaches to AG&T which, while not individualised are sufficiently open-ended to promote higher order thinking.

- Critical and creative thinking can be encouraged both separately and together as an aspect of higher-order provision.

- Provision may be through augmented schemes of work or newly planned schemes designed to encourage individualised learning.

6

Supporting AG&T outside the classroom

> **This chapter considers provision for AG&T learners outside the classroom, which can involve:**
>
> - A wide range of academic clubs and/or interest groups made available within an extended school day
> - Taking advantage of external providers, agencies, learning partnerships and the wider community to extend learning opportunities
> - The possibility of personalised provision for individual learners
> - Support for parents and carers in encouraging their AG&T youngsters
> - Bringing external learning opportunities into the classroom using ICT.

This chapter examines a range of opportunities for schools to support AG&T learners outside the taught curriculum. In this, the aim is to set out options for consideration when developing extra-curricular activities to enhance personalised learning programmes. In addition, attention is also given to the endeavour to assist parents of AG&T pupils in their role as partners in the learning process. The hope is to establish some principles of good practice in the selection, development, delivery and coordination of initiatives to expand and enrich the provision made for pupils in addition to that planned to deliver the common curriculum.

Out of class enrichment activities

As part of a curriculum of opportunity a school needs to consider its extra-curricular activities. In some areas the chance to develop significant skills is only possible on an extra-curricular level. Sport, drama and musical events are good examples of this approach whereby AG&T pupils get opportunities to excel in the school's sporting teams, theatrical productions or orchestras.

Such a model allows those with ability or talent in a particular field to have their needs met through extra-curricular activity while also allowing the opportunity for recreational enjoyment. A mathematics club featuring puzzles and investigations or a reading discussion group focusing on a common text, meeting at lunchtime or after school can provide similar opportunities for those pupils whose interests and aptitudes are less often met outside the classroom. Other examples might include: ICT clubs featuring virtual learning environments (VLEs); local history and/or geography fieldwork groups; science project teams working towards a specific problem-solving objective or competition entry (e.g. building a hydrofoil craft); art appreciation societies or comic-book drawing circles and design development teams working on producing, for example, an improved paper aeroplane.

Alternatively, enrichment in terms of extra-curricular interest groups may be developed along non-subject-specific lines. Examples of such provision with particular appeal to AG&T pupils could include:

- a chess club (or additionally/alternatively a Scrabble, Boggle or Go club)

- a debating society

- a philosophy group

- a word and number puzzle circle

- an astronomy or archaeology or palaeontology interest group

- a creative writing network or classical mythology club.

In this context, it is important that the focus of the provision should offer intellectual or developmental challenge but it is equally important that the staff involved in supporting the activity do so from a sense of personal commitment and enthusiasm. Teaching and other staff are powerful models in communicating their own interests and passions to young learners and giving a sense of legitimacy and enjoyment to intellectual pursuits can be as important as anything learned from the pursuits themselves in terms of helping to develop a youngster's sense of belonging to the world of ideas and joy through learning.

Other approaches are set out below.

A masterclass programme

Such provision normally features a series of specially targeted lessons/lectures outside of normal school hours delivered either by outside providers with particular expertise (perhaps through links with partner schools, community outreach programmes or further education institutions), or 'in-house' programmes delivered by teachers wishing to enhance challenge by developing a particular area of expertise. Such an approach – taken by a secondary school drawing on its subject specialists and specialist equipment to provide a learning boost for younger children – can also be a valuable means of developing primary/secondary links and supporting transition between phases. Experience also shows that schools which provide such opportunities reap practical benefits in terms of attracting larger numbers of AG&T entrants on transfer.

In addition many organisations run masterclass programmes for children which will be of interest to the gifted and talented. The British Science Association CREST awards, for example, offer a coherent programme of activities for after-school extension provision (see www.britishscienceassociation.org.uk). The Institute of Physics, also runs an annual programme of masterclass events (see www. particlephysics.ac.uk/teach/master-classes.html for details), while many arts institutions (such as The Theatre Royal http://www.masterclass.org.uk) offer a wide range of masterclass and other educational opportunities for children of all ages. At the time of writing, Bath University is offering a masterclass in banjo playing.

Saturday classes/clubs

Weekend classes offer the opportunity for children to work over a longer period of time on investigative and problem-solving challenges that need not be directly linked to the taught curriculum. Egg races, collaborative design competitions, thinking challenges and other open-ended learning experiences become possible. Additionally, Saturday classes allow for concentration on a particular talent or skill such as, for example, sculpture or book making or kite building or web page design or fossil collecting or any other activity to stimulate interest and broaden experience. Such events may also, of course, be subject-specific, designed to appeal to and challenge children with particular aptitudes in areas such as science or mathematics or art which are not often given extra-curricular time. Advantages of any or all such programmes are that they:

- Offer flexibility in terms of numbers attending and frequency of events

- Are less problematic to organise and accommodate than in curriculum time

- Allow for a more relaxed, experimental atmosphere for both teachers and learners

- Provide the opportunity to widen involvement outside of the school cohort, perhaps to feeder primary schools or to clusters of schools, thus providing opportunities to address the potential isolation of gifted children

- Make it easier to draw in parental and/or community-based expertise

- May be at least partly self-funding if parents are asked to make a voluntary contribution towards costs.

Trips, visits, curriculum events

Day trips and organised visits offer a wealth of opportunities to enrich and extend children's appreciation of their classwork. Indeed this is an area in which schools of all kinds have traditionally sought to offer a variety of learning and recreational experiences and there is a huge, almost bewildering, range of providers offering everything from afternoon museum visits to skiing holidays.

Indeed, in some cases the free availability of opportunities for educational visits can mean that these are planned in an ad hoc manner related to individual enthusiasms, contacts and traditions. An audit or annual report of such visits may then indicate an imbalance of provision in some areas over others. For example, a vigorous programme of theatre trips and theatre in education days, though laudable in itself, can expose a comparative paucity of wider cultural activity in, say, science and technology. Where this is the case, policy may seek to establish the principles of planning a balanced programme over any year or key stage. The same criteria can also apply to curriculum days or enhanced learning days when timetables are abandoned in favour of a whole-school focus on a particular area or skill-base. Thus, an autumn term book week could be set against a spring term mathematics challenge, a summer science and technology focus and an end-of-year problem-solving day.

Summer schools and transition events

In the UK summer schools for AG&T pupils have been promoted through educational funding streams (under a changing variety of headings and initiatives) for a number of years. There are broadly 3 types of event on offer:

- Those provided locally by individual schools or local learning networks

- Those offered regionally by universities and other learning institutions

- Residential events open to pupils on the national AG&T register through government-sponsored support organisations.

While the two latter events may be considered as personalised resources for individual high attainers, the former provides an opportunity for local settings to provide for a target group of their AG&T cohort. For example, one school near to London based the event (for 14-year-old pupils) around the concept of citizenship and used the resources of the capital city to conduct an investigation into the political structure and decision-making processes of central and local government. This focus, clearly developing leadership as well as academic skills, involved a visit to the Houses of Parliament and a meeting with the Prime Minister. Another summer school took geology as its theme. This involved many challenging and stimulating field visits and a final exhibition of fossils and rock samples to parents and invited guests. A third based the week-long event on a production of a *A Midsummer Night's Dream,* including set and costume design, make-up and lighting as well as directing and performance. Other activities, have focused on primary/secondary transition by offering one day a week induction over the summer period for AG&T pupils from all feeder primary schools.

In planning such events the following considerations should be borne in mind:

- Identification strategies should be transparent and nominations should clearly indicate the criteria used to make the selection

- Mixed age and mixed school cohorts offer valuable social opportunities and support, especially for those in primary/secondary transition

- Parents should be kept regularly and reliably informed of the summer school details and developments. Parental meetings can help. Consider developing opportunities for parents to work alongside their children in summer school learning activities

- School-based audit information, improvement plan objectives for AG&T and pupil self-assessments/planning input/surveys can be used to identify an appropriate focus for the event (i.e. ensure that it meets the school's and pupils' needs)

- Data from partner schools can be sought on pupils taking part to inform provision

- Pupils' involvement in their own performance assessment, and also that of the summer school overall should be allowed. Self-assessment encourages ownership

- A final event/production provides a focus for the summer school, offering opportunities for all involved to celebrate the achievements of the pupils and the programme. It can also be of value to the assessment procedure

- Opportunities should be developed for the good practice in teaching, learning, assessment and personalised provision promoted through the summer school to be celebrated and disseminated across the school to have a positive impact on teaching and learning for AG&T pupils generally. Ideally summer schools should not be a 'one off' event or a thinly disguised recruitment ploy, but should develop approaches/activities that have a continuation within the wider curriculum

- Finally, remember that this is a holiday period and – as with all extra-curricular events – ensure that the content is challenging, engaging and supportive of joy through learning. Relaxed stimulation is the appropriate note to aim for. AG&T children are still children and are as likely as any young person to respond negatively where content is perceived to be punitively laborious and/or dryly academic.

So far as transition is concerned, summer schools operating as staged events are not the only means of supporting movement from one phase of learning to the next. Secondary schools should consider holding an induction programme for their able pupils already identified through the primary school assessments or through SAT tests to clarify the opportunities open to the more able and to establish academic expectations and support for AG&T learners.

In view of evidence about the potential for children to make poor progress following transfer and the discontinuity in monitoring which may occur, it is a good policy to ensure that high-achieving children are provided with *bridging projects* or *challenges* set in primary schools and received by destination schools. Where such practice is planned, it is important that the work submitted is properly assessed, celebrated and used as part of the initial assessment and monitoring of the new AG&T cohort. Schools which have used bridging work but then failed to acknowledge the value of the pupils' efforts have found that the approach can disappoint and demoralise rather than energise youngsters who have taken the activity seriously as a way of revealing their abilities to their new teachers.

Personalised extra-curricular support

One implication of the personalised learning agenda is that new technology combined with the idea of flexible learning pathways matching individual need raise question marks about the traditionally understood boundaries of the school and its curriculum. Increasingly – and particularly with pupils of exceptional ability – schools will need to consider meeting the needs of individual pupils by aligning them to learning and support opportunities existing beyond the school walls and/or outside the general curriculum offer.

Mentoring for example has been found to be of proven benefit to gifted children who often value the opportunity to discuss their academic development with an adult who is able to provide an appropriate model and looked for direction, which may be unavailable at home or among peer groups. Overall academic mentoring is usually conducted by trained teachers or other professionals working within the school. *Personal mentors*, however, can (with appropriate checks) be recruited from the local community and linked to an individual pupil who might benefit significantly from meeting with an adult who has achieved success in a field of expertise in which the younger learner has potential and/or ambition. Such schemes should be:

- sustainable and consistent over a period of time

- clear to parents and pupils regarding objectives, procedures and schedules

- monitored to ensure that all parties are happy with the arrangement and that the pupil derives appropriate benefit from the support

- organised through the school with volunteer mentors supported/trained by a lead member of staff

- evaluated by both child and mentor to establish success and/or modify practice.

It is also important not to neglect the role of peer mentoring in which older AG&T students work with younger ones to support their learning and development within the school. This has proved to be a powerful way of providing support and challenge for both the mentor and the mentee within an overall focus on the power of student support for learning and student voice.

Other examples of personalised out-of-school and/or extra-curricular support for appropriate AG&T pupils can include:

- Out-of-school courses (for example at partner secondary schools or higher education institutions or specialist academies)

- More advanced online programmes or distance learning courses as offered by tutorial organisations or by the Open University

- Learning programmes or content from the internet produced outside the school made accessible through a VLE.

A virtual learning environment (such as Moodle) typically features:

- communication tools such as email, bulletin boards and chat rooms

- collaboration tools such as online forums, intranets, electronic diaries and calendars

- tools to create online content and courses

- online assessment and marking

- integration with school management information systems

- controlled access to curriculum resources

- student access to content and communications beyond the school.

Such features not only allow individual students the facility to discuss and collaborate with similar individuals or AG&T communities outside the school, but also to access online courses or content uploaded from other settings and educational institutions. In this it possible for pupils to be working outside the school while being physically inside the school, or (e.g. for homework or during holidays) to pursue learning programmes independently.

Clearly, the quality and range of such provision is constantly evolving and improving but the benefit of this approach to personalised provision is that schools and teachers do not need to abandon their academic guidance of learners to the unpredictability of online content. Rather a VLE allows teachers to create or upload their own content; trawl sites to identify appropriate material and post links to appropriate material either to target pupils or for more general use. Thus, to give one modest illustration of what can be done; a teacher might compile a virtual puzzle box of sites offering mental challenges (e.g. http://www. wordplays.com) and online interactive competitions to produce a twenty-first century equivalent to a classroom-based enrichment box providing appropriate challenge for AG&T pupils after they have completed their scheduled classwork.

Activity

Using the grid in Figure 6.1, conduct a preliminary audit of your school's current extra-curricular provision. Aim to evaluate this from the perspective of:

- overall curriculum and pastoral coverage (i.e. which area(s) of learning are covered well, which adequately and which are currently insufficiently supported)

- specific opportunities the provision currently provides for supporting AG&T learners

- which area(s) of extra-curricular support it would be most desirable (and most realistic) to develop with AG&T provision in mind.

Extra-curricular provision	Overall 0–5	AG&T 0–5	Areas to develop
Sport and psychomotor			
Music			
Drama			
Other academic areas			
Interest groups/clubs			
Masterclass (or other advanced input)			
Saturday classes			
Trips/visit programme			
Suspended curriculum/learning days			
Summer schools			
Transition support			
Personalised extra-curricular support			

Figure 6.1

A mark of zero indicates that no such provision exists. A mark of five means that provision is fully in place and its quality and impact on learners is judged to be outstanding. Three shows that provision is deemed to be broadly satisfactory in that area.

This activity is to prompt consideration of areas of provision to develop within the school or setting's overall improvement plan for AG&T. The initial aim is to brainstorm appropriate or desired developments. Clearly, further work will then be required in formulating an appropriate improvement plan to secure the objectives. A modified version of this activity (omitting the first 3 categories) can also be undertaken by individual departments or curriculum areas seeking to augment their own extra-curricular provision for AG&T learners.

Helping parents support their children's learning

For good or ill perhaps the most important extra-curricular influence on any child's learning is his/her home environment and the level of support and encouragement provided by parents and carers.

Support for parents and carers in their role as nurturers of ability and talent can take a number of forms. Broadly, however, schools and settings might wish to consider developing some or all of the following options.

Evidence gathering to inform subsequent support

On entry to a new school or phase of learning it is common for schools to meet with parents to discuss their perception of their child from the point of view of attitudes and behaviours towards learning. As a function of the school's identification procedure, it is wise at this point to allow parents to put forward their views regarding their child's perceived ability level and/or skill acquisition. Sometimes this form of nomination can be made through a formal document inviting carers to record their view of the child's potential and/or current level of achievement. A potential problem with such evidence gathering, however, is that not all parents are equipped to interpret their child's behaviour in terms of its relevance to educational outcomes. Indeed, research has shown that some parents may be inclined to interpret the behaviours of some AG&T children as problems rather than as signs of high ability. Alternatively, other parents may overestimate the potential of their child and place unreasonable expectations both on the youngster and on the school. In this context it is recommended that, wherever feasible, questions put to parents should form part of a dialogue with the school rather than simply be collected through the form of a questionnaire.

Such evidence gathering can be relatively generic:

- What activities does your child enjoy at home?

- What are his/her interests and hobbies?

- Did/does your child read before starting school?

- Have you noticed any special talents in your child?

It can, however, also seek to gain further insight into the youngster's likely capacity/ability as a learner against such indicators as:

- Thinks quickly

- Is curious/questioning

- Has a good memory

- Has a sense of humour

- Has many interests

- Likes to discuss 'mature' topics

- Likes being a leader, etc.

Clearly, such questions may readily be adapted to support parental interviews from the identification checklists examined earlier. Where a greater degree of precision is sought, it is even possible to ask parents to place their responses to such questions on a 0–5-point scale with 0 representing 'not at all'. Schools seeking a thoroughgoing interview format may even wish to introduce gradations of possible response to overarching indicators across a wide range of categories including:

- Questioning

- Memory

- Concentration

- Tolerance of failure or disappointment

- Vocabulary

- Language and communication skills

- Relations with peers, older children and adults

- Facility with numbers/numeracy skills

- General knowledge and interests

- Imagination

- Tenacity/ability in problem-solving

- Abstract thinking

- Lateral and creative thinking

- Reading

- Writing.

While such a number of categories seems inappropriate for most carers, exhaustive information-gathering of this sort may well be suitable for individual parents of identified AG&T pupils as part of a family-wide support package in which the school seeks to gain a more detailed profile of particular youngsters to inform targeted provision. In such cases the teacher or learning mentor conducting the interview should benefit from a more exhaustive list of sub-indicators under each main area of enquiry. For example, under the heading 'Lateral and creative thinking' there might be several prompts to guide both interviewer and parents towards a more precise response:

- Often/sometimes/never sees connections and links ideas (e.g. sees pictures in stains or patterns)

- Often/sometimes/never thinks or talks metaphorically

- Concentrates exclusively on one toy or activity at a time

- Does not happily combine or 'piggyback' ideas, seeming to think in more logical or linear ways

- Often/sometimes/never comes up with new or surprising ideas.

Once evidence is gathered and contact with parents made, decisions can then be made regarding the nature and extent of the support to be extended to parents either individually or as a group.

Ready availability of information, networking and parenting advice

As a minimum, the home-school handbook or prospectus or contact book or even website should contain basic information about the strategies the school uses to support AG&T pupils, with advice on how parents might support the school in its aims. Such advice on how to make best use of the school's provision and ethos around AG&T might also be expanded to include some appropriate general advice on parental good practice when caring for AG&T children. See for example, the list given in Figure 6.2.

Further approaches useful to parents in this area could include:

- Providing details of parental support agencies, community activities, sports and interest groups, summer schools, events promoted by the National Academy of Gifted and Talented Youth and/or local networks of AG&T parent-and-children groups such as those established throughout the UK by the National Association of Gifted Children (see www.nagcbritain.org.uk)

- Developing a section of the school website or VLE for parents, providing more detailed advice on support, events and resources. Where practicable, parents may even be given access to the pupil-level intranet or VLE to facilitate their support for the learning challenges and online communities available to pupils

- Allowing parents to attend academic monitoring, progress reviews and/or target-setting sessions to better enable their ongoing support of improvement objectives

Advice for parents and carers of able, gifted and talented children

- Encourage children to ask questions and answer them fully and honestly.

- Admit to uncertainty when you do not have a full answer.

- Encourage fantasy and imagination as much as the pursuit of knowledge.

- Encourage experimentation, showing that failure in this context is no disgrace.

- Give children the opportunity to evaluate their own work and behaviour.

- Encourage the expression of fears and anxieties and discuss these supportively.

- Share play but also make room for solitary play/hobbies.

- Encourage contentment with incomplete knowledge/understanding.

- Allow open discussion but do not give up responsibility for making decisions.

- Allow discussion of all subjects and encourage personal decision-making when appropriate.

- Use adult language structures and vocabulary in conversation with children.

- Beware of pressurising the child and treating him/her differently to siblings.

- Encourage the child to recognise that performance will always differ according to circumstances/subject, etc. and that this is OK.

- Give the emotional support to make him/her feel good about being different.

- Encourage tact, tolerance and understanding of others without similar abilities.

- Use community facilities (e.g. museums, galleries, concert halls, sport venues) to give opportunities to satisfy his/her thirst for knowledge and experience.

- Encourage the love of reading by giving, where possible, access to a wide variety of books and to the local library.

- Where possible give your child access to educational games/toys/musical instruments/computers and other practical equipment to allow the development of a broad range of skills and talents.

- Try to arrange contact with other more able children and with adults who have expertise/interest in any area where a child shows signs of aptitude.

- Where possible travel with your child to make the most of opportunities offered by the school and the community.

- FINALLY and importantly, ensure that your child is not subjected to undue work and pressure and has the time to RELAX, ENJOY LIFE and BE A CHILD!

Figure 6.2

- Setting up and accommodating a parents' group to facilitate involvement in classroom support, mentoring, extra-curricular programmes, etc. and also to share information on parenting, resources and collaborative self-help

- Making links with local-authority sponsored parenting courses to refer individual parents who are particularly challenged by looking after an AG&T youngster.

Develop guidelines and advice on how to support pupils at home

Following on from general advice on parenting and relationships, some schools may identify the need to provide parents with detailed guidance on family-based activities designed to interest and motivate receptive young minds. Such a publication or website should contain suggested ways of helping to nurture potential without such activities feeling punitive or laborious. The nature of the advice will, of course, vary with the age and needs of the cohort but could include activities such as the following:

- Play Scrabble or Boggle together (for older or more advanced players consider using only words related to a theme – e.g. holidays or sport).

- Invent 10 new uses for a household item. Alternatively improve the design of something in common use such as a waste bin or dishmop or even a pet.

- Compare a foreign-language newspaper, magazine, pop record or comic book with an English version. Plan/problem-solve itineraries, etc. for your next foreign holiday or else an ideal tour and cook a related ethnic dish.

- Involve children in real-life consumer issues by writing letters/emails to manufacturers complaining about or endorsing products or making suggestions and designing improvements. Discuss advertisements for obvious and hidden messages and create a new, perhaps more truthful, jingle. Enter a manufacturer's competition together.

- Investigate and enrich the family identity. Have an older family member discuss life 50 years ago. Design/make a family crest or flag or seal depicting family history and symbols of the family values. Prepare a motto to accompany this design. Research and illustrate the family tree. Keep a diary or photo-diary or online montage of family events and give each section a particular tone or style, for example, a poem/a newspaper headline, etc. Produce a family web page or blog.

- Investigate and record (video camera, digital photographs, audio, sketchbook, etc.) a feature of domestic life, for example, body language, animal communication, speech, etc.

- Develop and use your own family communication practices. This could involve anything from invented words for common items or events and new systems of body language and gesture, to family-based sign language or even new language systems for particular situations (e.g. dinner talk).

- Have the child redesign/help redecorate his/her bedroom to accommodate his/her hobbies and interests – design the ideal bedroom.

- Play various types of music (e.g. jazz, reggae, classical, pop) and discuss mood, style, technique, etc. Encourage free dance expression to each.

- Discuss a favourite TV programme and plan two new plots/sub-plots for the characters. Discuss the plausibility of current plots and how they could be improved.

- Watch sport and invent a new one. Make up appropriate rules, uniforms and equipment, etc.

- Examine local newspapers for local problems and plan logical solutions. Write letters to the editor over matters of concern or interest.

- Learn a craft or interest-related art form (e.g. Temari and mathematics).

- Condense a film, book or TV programme into four sentences (or four words). Whose version is best?

- Create and illustrate a new cartoon strip with a new hero/heroine.

- Devise and set up a home weather station for recording conditions. Set up a database to record and plot the information.

- Examine advice and plan ways of making the house more environmentally friendly. Design systems for conserving water and/or energy.

- Read the same book together and discuss it as a family.

- Investigate online communities/interest groups and contribute to the discussion boards, chat rooms, etc.

- Learn together about particular types of plants, vegetables or herbs. Plan a garden or bed together including a new garden layout, a timetable for planting, flowering/watering, etc. Tend the area as a family project.

- Plan simple chemical experiments and discuss the chemical components in household items and food.

- Solve crossword puzzles, anagrams, riddles, acrostics, sudoku, kakuro and other number puzzles together, then construct your own for others to solve.

- Explore areas of the house for unused items or 'antiques'. Discuss their value against economic concepts such as appreciation/depreciation. Have the children plan/participate in a car boot sale or eBay auction.

- Play strategy games such as chess, drafts, backgammon, Go, etc. Graduate to participate in online games in leagues as part of family competition.

Activity

Use the information in this chapter and elsewhere to plan a parental support booklet or web page for the carers of AG&T pupils in your school. Decide on:

- format and design
- the range of content required to meet perceived need
- a timescale and/or action plan for development, production and launch.

As a planning activity this should take 30 minutes. More time may be allocated where development groups are working on the draft of a proposed document.

To think about

- What capacity does the school have to extend its current extra-curricular provision for AG&T?
- What safeguards and/or monitoring will be necessary if the school is to ensure children's safety and well-being during extra-curricular activities?
- How does the notion of using ICT/VLEs to bring external learning programmes into the classroom impact on the school's current understanding of teaching, learning and curriculum delivery?
- To what extent is the development of parental partnerships and support a priority for the school with regard to its most able learners?

Summary

Some key points and suggestions have been made in this chapter in relation to supporting AG&T outside the classroom.

- Schools should evaluate the range and nature of the provision for learning offered outside the taught curriculum.
- Extra-curricular provision may also be offered through developing community links to support learning.
- Parents of AG&T should be supported as partners in their children's learning and given practical advice/activities to challenge and engage their youngster.

Appendix

Goldilocks and the Three Bears

The three bears lived in a house in the forest. There was a father bear, a mother bear and a baby bear. Mother bear was big enough but father bear was even bigger and more scary, especially when he showed his long sharp claws and huge fangs.

In the bears' house there were three chairs. The biggest chair was father bear's. The smallest chair was baby bear's. There were also three bowls. There was a very big bowl for father bear, a smaller bowl for mother bear and a little bowl for baby bear. Upstairs there were three beds. Father bear had a great big bed. Mother bear had a smaller bed, and baby bear had a tiny little bed.

One day, mother bear made some porridge for breakfast. She put it in the three bowls on the table. But the porridge was too hot to eat, so father bear said that they should go for a walk in the forest until it cooled down.

A little girl called Goldilocks lived at the edge of the forest near to the bears' house. Her mother said that she was not allowed to go into the forest alone but that morning she decided to walk through the trees to find somewhere new to play. She saw the bears' house and wanted to see who lived there. She knocked at the door but no one answered. She pushed open the door and went inside.

She was hungry so she tried a spoonful of father bear's porridge but it was still too hot. Then she ate some of mother bear's porridge but it was too salty. Then she tried some of baby bear's porridge and it was just right. So she gobbled it all up.

Next she sat on father bear's chair but it was too high. She sat on mother bear's chair but it was too lumpy. Then she sat on baby bear's chair and it was just right. But Goldilocks was too heavy for the chair and it broke.

After that she went upstairs. She was tired, so she lay on father bear's giant bed but it was too hard. Then she lay on mother bear's bed but it was too soft. Finally Goldilocks got into baby bear's bed and it was just right, so she closed her eyes and went to sleep.

When the three bears came back from their walk in the forest father bear looked at his bowl and roared, 'someone's been eating my porridge'. Mother bear looked at her bowl and added more calmly, 'someone's been eating my porridge too'. Then baby bear cried, 'someone's been eating my porridge and eaten it all up!'

When they saw their chairs, father and mother bear could tell that someone had been sitting in them and father growled angrily showing his fierce teeth. But baby bear said tearfully, 'someone's been sitting in my chair and broken it to pieces'.

Rushing upstairs, father bear was furious. 'Someone's been sleeping in my bed', he snarled. 'Someone's been sleeping in my bed too,' said mother bear, more shocked than angry. But when baby bear gasped, 'someone's been sleeping in my bed and she's still there', all the bears howled in surprise, father bellowing loudest of all.

All this noise woke Goldilocks and she was frightened to see the three bears staring at her with their mouths wide open. Without a word, she got out of bed and ran down the stairs, out of the house and back to her own house. Mother bear cleaned the bedroom and made some more porridge while father bear made baby bear a new chair. Goldilocks never came back and the three bears never saw her again.

Useful websites, agencies and associations

Schools may wish to align themselves with (or direct parents towards) some of the following agencies concerned with promoting gifted and talented education:

Brunel Able Children's Education (BACE) Centre
Centre Director: Professor Valsa Koshy. Email: Valsa.Koshy@brunel.ac.uk
Brunel Able Children's Education Centre
Brunel University
School of Sport and Education
Halsbury Building (Room 102)
Uxbridge
Middlesex
UB8 3PH
Tel: +44 (0)1895 267164. Fax: +44 (0)1895 269806
BACE website: www.brunel.ac.uk/about/acad/sse/sseres/sseresearchcentres/bacehome

The BACE Centre was launched in 1997 within the School of Education at Twickenham and undertakes research and provides evidence-based strategies for both policy-makers and practitioners. The BACE team contributes at national and international conferences and works with a large network of Local Authorities and schools, providing research-based strategies and systems for evaluating provision for gifted and talented students.

The Hong Kong Academy for Gifted Education
East Block
Kowloon Tong Education Services Centre
19 Suffolk Rd
Kowloon Tong
Hong Kong
Tel: +853 3698 4103. Fax: +852 3586 3445
Email: academy@hkage.org.hk
HKAGE website: http://hkage.org.hk/en/index.html

The academy provides challenging learning opportunities for gifted students to enable them to stretch their potential in a wide range of specialist areas, including leadership, creativity, personal-social competence. All the courses are available 'off site', though school venues will not be uncommon. The website provides information and resources for students, parents and teachers.

MENSA
British Mensa Ltd
St John's House
St John's Square

Wolverhampton
WV2 4AH
Tel: +44 (0) 1902 772 771. Fax: +44 (0) 1902 392 500
MENSA website: www.mensa.org.uk

MENSA is a registered charity (No. 00971663) for people with a high IQ. It provides a range of activities, social networks and research opportunities for members. Its website offers support, IQ testing and mental challenges for adults and children.

The National Association for Able Children in Education (NACE)
Chief Executive: Julie Fitzpatrick
NACE National Office
PO Box 242
Arnolds Way
Oxford
OX2 9FR
Tel: +44 (0)1865 861879. Fax: +44 (0)1865 861880
Email: info@nace.co.uk
NACE website: www.nace.co.uk

NACE is a registered charity (No. 327320) and is the UK's largest independent organisation supporting teachers, schools, local authorities and wider agencies in their work with AG&T learners. It has an extensive network of member schools and individual teachers throughout the UK, organises a wide range of conference and CPD opportunities, has developed (in conjunction with Oxford Brookes University) the NACE Challenge Award kitemark and self-review standard and publishes a wide range of resources for use in schools. NACE membership and services and publications can be accessed through its website.

The National Association for Gifted Children
NAGC
Suite 14
Challenge House
Sherwood Drive
Bletchley
Milton Keynes
Buckinghamshire
MK3 6DP
Tel: +44 (0)845 450 0295. Fax: +44 (0)870 770 3219
Email: amazingchildren@nagcbritain.org.uk
Website: www.nagcbritain.org.uk

The NAGC is a registered charity working on behalf of talented children and their families. Parents or organisations may join and a range of services are offered including counselling. It has a network of local branches that organise activities for children in the area. It has several publications for parents which may be accessed through the website.

The National Society for the Gifted and Talented
Membership Director: Emilia Musella
National Society for the Gifted & Talented™
River Plaza
9 West Broad Street
Stamford
CT 06902–3788
USA
Tel: (800) 572 6748. Fax: (203) 399 5590
Email: emusella@nsgt.org
Website: www.nsgt.org

NSGT is committed to acknowledging and supporting the needs of AG&T children
and youth through recognition of their significant academic and artistic accomplishments and by providing access to educational resources and advanced
learning opportunities directly related to their interests and talent areas.

Ohio Association for Gifted Children
501 Morrison Rd
Suite 103
Columbus
Ohio
43230
USA
Tel: +1 614 337 0386. Fax: +1 614 337 9286
Website: www.oagc.com

OAGC promotes and supports the development of gifted students through dis-
semination of information, advocacy on their behalf, encouragement of affiliate
organisations, and promotes research and education for gifted children.

Oxford Brookes University
Westminster Institute of Education
Harcourt Hill Campus
Oxford
England
OX2 9AT
Tel: +44 (0)1865 488600
Email: Ewioe@brookes.ac.uk
Web: www.brookes.ac.uk/schools/education/rescon/cpdgifted/home.html

OBU provides a wide range of information, resources, courses and professional
development materials for AG&T.

The Queensland Association for Gifted and Talented Children
QAGTC Inc.
PO Box 3246
Stafford DC

Queensland 4053
282 Stafford Rd
Stafford
Brisbane
Australia
Tel: (07) 3352 4288. Fax: (07) 3352 4388
Email: office@qagtc.org.au
Website: www.qagtc.org.au

QAGTC is an association for children, teachers/professionals and parents and offers a full range of support and advocacy services including educational training events, publications and membership services which may be accessed through the website.

The Sutton Trust
111 Upper Richmond Road
Putney
London
SW15 2TJ
Tel: +44 (0)20 8788 3223. Fax: 020 8788 3993
Email: james.turner@suttontrust.com
Website: www.suttontrust.com

The Sutton Trust is particularly concerned with breaking the link between educational opportunities and family background. Its projects include independent/state school partnerships and university summer schools.

World Council for Gifted and Talented Children
Headquarters
World Council for Gifted and Talented Children, Inc.
c/o The University of Winnipeg
515 Portage Avenue
Winnipeg
Manitoba
Canada R3B 2E9
Tel: 204 789 1421. Fax: 204 783 1188
Email: headquarters@world-gifted.org
Website: https://world-gifted.org/

WCGTC is a worldwide non-profit organisation whose primary goal is to provide advocacy and support for gifted children. It organises The World Conference through a membership of educators, scholars, researchers, parents and educational institutions.

Some useful forums, blogs and online communities for AG&T

American Gifted Education Blog
http://blogs.edweek.org/teachers/unwrapping_the_gifted/

Cogito – connecting young thinkers around the world (Johns Hopkins University)
www.cogito.org

Edublogs – online communities for teachers and students
http://edublogs.org/

Gifted families – a place to share ideas and insights from around the world
http://au.groups.yahoo.com/group/giftedfamilies/

Parents Centre on Department for Children, Schools and Families site UK
www.standards.dcsf.gov.uk/jiveforums/index.jspa?categoryID=65

Radiowaves global communications network for talented children
www.radiowaves.co.uk/

Times Educational Supplement discussion boards (search for AG&T)
www.tes.co.uk/forums.aspx

United Kingdom National Strategies and government agencies

CfBT Education Trust manages the Young Gifted and Talented programme excellence hubs established in nine English regions to provide a diverse range of outreach provision to gifted and talented learners including master classes, specialist subject activities and blended/online learning throughout and outside of the school year.
www.cfbt.com/teach/giftedtalentededucation/excellencehubs.aspx

Go to http://nationalstrategies.standards.dcsf.gov.uk and search for AG&T to select from an extensive range of guidance, resource information and e-learning modules compiled and promoted by The Department for Children Schools and Families.

The Qualifications and Curriculum Authority website has guidance on teaching and assessing AG&T pupils.
http://www.qca.org.uk/qca_2346.aspx

The Gifted and Talented area of the Standards Site outlines support strategies, identification issues and provides links to other agencies and NGOs supporting AG&T.
www.standards.dfes.gov.uk/giftedandtalented/

Teachernet provides the latest information and news related to AG&T learners.
www.teachernet.gov.uk/teachingandlearning/gandtpupils/

General resources and useful websites

The 21st Century Learning Initiative
//www.21learn.org/

Aquila magazine (8–13 year olds)
www.aquila.co.uk/

BBC Schools Online
www.bbc.co.uk/education/schools/

Bloom's Taxonomy and Learning Domains
www.businessballs.com/bloomstaxonomyoflearningdomains.htm

Cognitive Acceleration through Science Education (CASE) and Cognitive Acceleration through Maths Education (CAME)
www.kcl.ac.uk/schools/sspp/education/research/projects/case.html
www.kcl.ac.uk/schools/sspp/education/research/projects/came.html

Creative Learning Journey site
www.creativelearningjourney.org.uk/home.htm

Critical and Creative Thinking
http://eduscapes.com/tap/topic69.htm

Critical Thinking Community
www.criticalthinking.org/

Critical Thinking Overview
http://chiron.valdosta.edu/whuitt/col/cogsys/critthnk.html

Critical Thinking Skills in Education and Life
www.asa3.org/ASA/education/think/critical.htm

Gifted Students and the Socratic Method
http://teaching-gifted-students.suite101.com/article.cfm/socratic_method_and_gifted_students

Home Learning and Learning Styles
http://homeschooling.gomilpitas.com/weblinks/assets.htm

Independent Thinking and Multiple Intelligence Theory/questioning
www.independentthinking.co.uk/Cool+Stuff/8Way+Thinking/default.aspx

Kidsource site with summaries and links to AG&T resources and articles
www.kidsource.com/kidsource/pages/ed.gifted.html

Leadership, human motovation & research programmes
www.transforminglearning.co.uk/

Learning and Thinking provision for G&T
www.teachingexpertise.com/articles/inclusive-gifted-talented-provision-195

Learning Styles – About.com site
http://712educators.about.com/gi/dynamic/offsite.htm?zi=1/XJ/Ya&sdn=
712educators&cdn=education&tm=37&f=00&tt=14&bt=0&bts=1&st=32&zu=http
%3A//www.geocities.com/%257Eeducationplace/ls.html

Learning Styles BBC Wales Home Education, The Learning Gate
www.bbc.co.uk/wales/schoolgate/helpfromhome/content/2howchildrenlearn.shtml

Learning Styles inventory
www.oswego.edu/plsi/16TYPE.htm

Multiverse: exploring diversity and achievement in the UK educational context
www.multiverse.ac.uk

New South Wales Association for Gifted and Talented Children Inc
http://nswagtc.org.au/index.php

Post-16 G&T policy
www.dsfc.org.uk/gifted.htm

Queensland Gifted Education Site
www.learningplace.com.au/default_suborg.asp?orgid=23&suborgid=158

SAPERE, The Society for Advancing Philosophical Enquiry and Reflection in
Education
www.sapere.org.uk/

Schools' Resources
http://intele4.essex.ac.uk/Internet%20Resources/UK/subject.htm

Schools site with discussion forum and information
//www.schoolsnet.com/

Socratic Questioning – Changing Minds site
http://changingminds.org/techniques/questioning/socratic_questions.htm

Socratic Questioning – Starting Point site
http://serc.carleton.edu/introgeo/socratic/

Talented and Gifted Educational Resources
www.uis.edu/~schroede/school/taglink.htm

Teaching Ideas for Primary Teachers
www.teachingideas.co.uk/

Thinking Styles and Learning Styles CENGAGE Learning site
http://college.hmco.com/instructors/ins_teachtech_foundations_module_
thinkstyles.html

Virtual Learning Environments – BECTA site and download
http://partners.becta.org.uk/index.php?section=rh&rid=13640

Wise Ones: Nurturing High Potential
www.wiseones.com.au/Home/tabid/36/Default.aspx

Identification and assessment – useful websites

Creative Generation guidance on talent identification
http://ygt.dcsf.gov.uk/Content.aspx?contentId=185&contentType=3

Creativity – what is it? QCA site
http://curriculum.qca.org.uk/key-stages-1-and-2/learning-across-the-curriculum/creativity/whatiscreativity/index.aspx

Defining Giftedness – National Society for Giftedness & Talent site
www.nsgt.org/articles/index.asp

Defining Giftedness – Rhode Island Advocates for Gifted Education
www.riage.org/gifteddef.html

Definitions of gifted and talented – Hertfordshire Grid for Learning
www.thegrid.org.uk/learning/gifted/policies/definition.shtml

Definitions of giftedness and talent – National Literacy Trust site
www.literacytrust.org.uk/database/able.html

E-learning module on identification
www.nationalstrategiescpd.org.uk/course/view.php?id=81

Giftedness and the gifted – identification checklists Kidsource site
www.kidsource.com/kidsource/content/giftedness_and_gifted.html

Innate Talent – Psychology Today
www.psychologytoday.com/blog/beautiful-minds/200806/innate-talent-0

Is every child gifted? Probably not – Psychology Today
www.psychologytoday.com/blog/beautiful-minds/200805/is-every-child-gifted-probably-not-0

Talented performance: a Chinese model – Gifted Child Quarterly
http://gcq.sagepub.com/cgi/content/abstract/49/3/231

What is a gifted child? Definitions and links
http://nswagtc.org.au/info/definitions/

Who is gifted and talented? Standards Site definition
www.standards.dfes.gov.uk/giftedandtalented/who/

World Class Tests for Gifted and Talented
www.worldclassarena.org/v5/default.htm

Bibliography

Websites and downloads

All Our Futures: Creativity, Culture and Education
www.cypni.org.uk/downloads/alloutfutures.pdf

Bloom's taxonomy and classroom reading
www.ops.org/reading/blooms_taxonomy.html

English proverbs and sayings
www.learn-english-today.com/Proverbs/proverbs_L-Z.html

Fairy stories and traditional tales
www.primaryresources.co.uk/english/englishC4.htm

Fairy tales and jokes
www.jokelibrary.net/xOtherAtoM/fairy_tales.html

Folklore and mythology
www.pitt.edu/~dash/folktexts.html#g

John Donne: A Valediction Forbidding Mourning
www.luminarium.org/sevenlit/donne/mourning.php

Read and talk about stories
http://education.qld.gov.au/corporate/newbasics/html/richtasks/year3/resourcesrt
4.html

Similes from 'Said What'
www.saidwhat.co.uk/spoon/similes.php

Simile Generator
www.vigoschools.org/~mjm3/activities/simile.htm

Stimulate Higher Order Thinking with the random simile generator
www.nicksenger.com/blog/stimulate-higher-thinking-with-the-simile-generator

Word games
www.wordplays.com/p/index

UK Government publications and downloads

Classroom Quality Standards (CQS) guided resource is an online tool, to support self-evaluation and improvement in classroom provision, with guidance and exemplification.
www.standards.dcsf.gov.uk/nationalstrategies

Developing school policy for AG&T
www.nc.uk.net/gt/general/02_ wholeschool.htm

Early Years Foundation Stage Pack
http://publications.teachernet.gov.uk/default.aspx?PageFunction=
viewtoptenproducts&PageMode=publications&Type=TopTen&

Every Child Matters
www.everychildmatters.gov.uk/

Excellence and Enjoyment: Learning and Teaching in the Primary Years
http://publications.teachernet.gov.uk/default.aspx?PageFunction=productdetails
&PageMode=publications&ProductId=DfES+0344+2004&

Extended Services
www.teachernet.gov.uk/wholeschool/extendedschools

G&T wise resources
www.teachernet.gov.uk/gtwise

Gifted and Talented Education: Guidance on Addressing Underachievement: Planning a Whole-School Approach (June 2009)
http://publications.teachernet.gov.uk/default.aspx?PageFunction=viewlatest
additionstocatalogue&PageMode=publications&Type=LatestAdditions&

Gifted and Talented Education: Guidance on Preventing Underachievement: A Focus on Exceptionally Able Pupils
www.standards.dcsf.gov.uk/nationalstrategies
Search, using the reference '00066–2008BKT-EN'.

Identifying gifted and talented learners – getting started
London gifted and talented e-resources
www.londongt.org

National Curriculum AG&T guidance
www.nc.uk.net/gt/index.html
www.qca.org.uk/10012.html

National Quality Standards for Gifted and Talented Education
www.teachernet.gov.uk/gtwise

New relationship with schools
www.teachernet.gov.uk/newrelationship

Ofsted interactive site on self-evaluation
www.ofsted.gov.uk/schools

Personalised Learning – A Practical Guide (October 2008)
http://publications.teachernet.gov.uk/default.aspx?PageFunction=viewtopten
products&PageMode=publications&Type=TopTen&

Quality Standards (Institutional and Classroom)
www.standards.dcsf.gov.uk/nationalstrategies

Raiseonline information
www.ofsted.gov.uk/schools/dataandinformationsystems.cfm

Subject-specific teaching materials
www.teachernet.gov.uk/teachingandlearning/subjects/

Welsh Quality Standards document and download
Meeting the Challenge: Quality Standards in Education for More Able and Talented Pupils
(May 2008), Welsh Assembly Government Circular 006/2008
http://new.wales.gov.uk/publications/circular/2008/meetingthechallenge/?lang=en

Bibliography

Adey, P. (1991) 'Pulling yourself up by your own thinking', *European Journal for High Ability*, 2: 28–34.

Albert, R.S. (ed.) (1992) *Genius and Eminence: the Social Psychology of Creativity and Exceptional Achievement* (2nd edn). Oxford: Pergamon Press.

Ari, B.A. and Rich, Y. (1992) 'Meeting the educational needs of all students in the heterogeneous class', in P.S. Klein and A.J. Tannenbaum (eds) *To Be Young and Gifted*. New Jersey: Ablex Publishing.

Benbow, C.P. (1991) 'Meeting the needs of gifted students through use of acceleration', in M.C. Wang, M.C. Reynolds and H.J. Walberg (eds) *Handbook of Special Education*. Vol. 2. New York: Pergamon Press.

Berry, C. (1990) 'On the origins of exceptional intellectual and cultural achievement', in Michael J.A. Howe (ed.) *Encouraging the Development of Exceptional Skills and Talents*. Leicester: British Psychological Society.

Bloom, B. (1956) *Taxonomy of Educational Objectives: the Classification of Educational Goals, Handbook 1: Cognitive Domains*. Boston, MA: Allyn and Bacon.

Bloom, B. (ed.) (1985) *Developing Talent in Young People*. New York: Basic Books.

Butler-Por, N. (1993) 'Underachieving gifted students', in K.A. Heller, F.J. Monks and A.H. Passow, *International Handbook of Research and Development of Giftedness and Talent*. Oxford: Pergamon Press.

Casey, R. and Koshy, V. (1995) *Bright Challenges*. Cheltenham: Stanley Thornes.

Clark, C. and Callow, F. (1998) *Educating Able Children*. London: David Fulton.

Chyriwsky, M. and Kennard, R. (1997) 'Attitudes to able children: a survey of mathematics teachers in English secondary schools', *High Ability Studies*, 8: 47–59.

Colangelo, N. and Assouline, S. (1995) 'Self-concept of gifted students: patterns by self-concept domain, grade level, and gender', in M.W. Katzko and F.J. Monks (eds.) *Nurturing Talent: Individual Needs and Social Ability*. Assen, The Netherlands: Van Gorcum.

Cornell, D.G., Callahan, C.M., Bassin, L.E. and Ramsay, S.G. (1991) 'Affective development in accelerated students', in W. T. Southern and E.D. Jones (eds) *The Academic Acceleration of Gifted Children*. New York: Teacher's College.

Cox, J., Daniel, N. and Boston, B.A. (1985) *Educating Able Learners: Programs and Promising Practices*. Austin: University of Texas Press.

Cropley, A.J. (1995) 'Creative intelligence: a concept of "true" giftedness', in J. Freeman, P. Span and H. Wagner (eds) *Actualising Talent: a Life-span Approach*. London: Cassell.

Dar, Y. and Resh, N. (1986) *Classroom Composition and Pupil Achievement: A Study of the Effects of Ability-based Classes*. London: Gordon and Breach.

Deane, G. (1999) *Challenging the More Able Language User*. London: Fulton.

de Bono, Edward (1990) *Six Thinking Hats*. London: Penguin.

Denton, C. and Postlethwaite, K. (1985) *Able Children: Identifying them in the Classroom*. Windsor: NFER-Nelson.

Department for Children, Schools and Families (DCSF) (2008) *Identifying Gifted and Talented Learners – Getting Started*. Nottingham: Department for Children, Schools and Families.

Department for Children, Schools and Families (DCSF) (2009) *Your Child, Your Schools, Our Future: Building a 21st Century Schools System*. London: The Stationery Office.

Department for Children, Education, Lifelong Learning and Skills (2008) *Meeting the Challenge: Quality Standards in Education for More Able and Talented Pupils*. Welsh

Assembly Government Circular No. 006/2008, May. NACE.

Department for Education (1993) *Exceptionally Able Children.* London: Department for Education.

Department for Education and Employment (DfEE) (1999) *All Our Futures: Creativity, Culture and Education.* London: DfEE.

Elshout, J. (1995) 'Talent: the ability to become an expert', in J. Freeman, P. Span and H. Wagner (eds) *Actualizing Talent: a Lifelong Challenge.* London: Cassell.

Emerick, L.J. (1992), 'Academic underachievement among the gifted: students perceptions of factors that reverse the pattern', *Gifted Child Quarterly*, 36: 140–6.

Ericsson, K.A. and Lehman, A.C. (1996) 'Expert and exceptional performance: evidence of maximal adaptation to task constraints', *Annual Review of Psychology*, 47: 273–305.

Eyre, D. (1997) *Able Children in Ordinary Schools.* London: David Fulton.

Eyre, D. and Lowe, H. (2002) *Educating Able Children.* London: David Fulton.

Eyre, D. and McClure, L. (2001) *Curriculum Provision for the Gifted and Talented in the Primary School.* London: David Fulton.

Eysenck, H.J. (1995) *Genius: the Natural History of Creativity.* Cambridge: Cambridge University Press.

Feldhusen, J.F. and Kroll, M.D. (1991) 'Boredom or challenge for the academically talented in school', *Gifted Education International*, 7: 80–1.

Feuerstein, R. and Tannenbaum, A.J. (1993) 'Mediating the learning experience of gifted underachievers', in B. Wallace and H.B. Adams (eds) *Worldwide Perspectives on the Gifted Disadvantaged.* Bicester: AB Academic Publishers.

Fisher, R. (1992) *Teaching Children to Think.* Cheltenham: Stanley Thornes.

Fisher R. (1995) *Teaching Children to Learn.* Cheltenham: Stanley Thornes.

Fisher R. (1998) *Teaching Thinking.* London: Cassell.

Freeman, J. (1991) *Gifted Children Growing Up.* London: Cassell; Portsmouth, NJ: Heinemann Educational.

Freeman, J. (1992) 'Boredom, high ability and underachievement', in V. Varma (ed.) *How and Why Children Fail.* London: Jessica Kingsley.

Freeman, J. (1993) 'Parents and families in nurturing giftedness and talent', in K.A. Heller, F.J. Monks and A.H. Passow (eds) *International Handbook for Research on Giftedness and Talent.* Oxford: Pergamon Press.

Freeman, J. (1995) 'Towards a policy for actualizing talent', in J. Freeman, P. Span and H. Wagner (eds) *Actualizing Talent: a Lifelong Challenge.* London: Cassell.

Freeman, J. (1996) *Highly Able Girls and Boys.* London: Department for Education and Employment.

Freeman, J. (1997) 'The emotional development of the highly able', *European Journal of Psychology in Education*, XII: 479–93.

Freeman, J. (1998) 'Mentoring gifted pupils', in S. Goodlad (ed.) *Mentoring and Tutoring by Students.* London: Kogan Page.

Gagné, F. (1985) 'Giftedness and talent', *Gifted Child Quarterly*, 29: 103–12.

Gagné, F. (1995) 'Learning about the nature of gifts and talents through peer and teacher nominations', in M.W. Katzko and F.J. Monks (eds) *Nurturing Talent: Individual Needs and Social Ability.* Assen, The Netherlands: Van Gorcum.

Gagné, F. (2004) 'Transforming gifts into talents', *High Ability Studies*, 15(2): 119–47.

Gallagher, J., Harraine, C.C. and Coleman, M.R. (1997) 'Challenge or boredom? Gifted students' views on their schooling'. *Roeper Review*, 19: 132–6.

Galloway, G. (1994) 'Psychological studies of the relationship of sense of humour to creativity and intelligence: a review', *European Journal for High Ability*, 5: 133–44.

Gardner, H. (1983) *Frames of Mind: the Theory of Multiple Intelligences.* New York: Basic Books.

Gardner, H. (1993) *Creating Minds: an Anatomy of Creativity Seen Through the Lives of Freud, Einstein, Picasso, Stravinsky, Eliot, Graham, and Gandhi.* New York: Basic Books.

Gardner, H. (1994) *The Creator's Pattern*, in M.A. Boden (ed.) *Dimensions of Creativity*. Cambridge, MA: Massachusetts Institute of Technology.

Gardner, H. (1997) *Extraordinary Minds*. London: Weidenfeld and Nicolson.

Gardner, H. (1999) *Intelligence Reframed: Multiple Intelligences for the 21st Century*. New York: Basic Books.

Gardner, H. (2006) *Multiple Intelligences: New Horizons*. New York: Basic Books.

Geake, J. (2009) *The Brain at School: Educational Neuroscience in the Classroom*. London: Open University Press.

George, D. (1992) *The Challenge of the Able Child*. London: David Fulton.

Gross, M.U.M. (1993) 'Nurturing the talents of exceptionally gifted individuals', in K.A. Heller, F.J. Monks and A.H. Passow (eds) *International Handbook of Research and Development of Giftedness and Talent*. Oxford: Pergamon Press.

Hansen, J.B. and Feldhusen, J.F. (1994) 'Comparison of trained and untrained teachers of gifted students', *Gifted Child Quarterly*, 38: 115–21.

Hany, E.A. (1993) 'How teachers identify gifted students: feature processing or concept based classification', *European Journal for High Ability*, 4: 196–211.

Heller, K.A. and Hany, E.A. (1995) 'German–Chinese study on technical creativity: cross-cultural perspectives', paper presented at the World Council for Gifted and Talented Children meeting in Hong Kong.

Her Majesty's Inspectorate (HMI) (1992) *The Education of Very Able Children in Maintained Schools. A Review by HMI*. London: HMSO.

Johnson, L.J. and Lewman, B.S. (1990) 'Parents' perceptions of the talents of young gifted boys and girls', *Journal for the Education of the Gifted*, 13: 176–88.

Jonassen, D.H. (2000) *Computers as Mindtools for Schools: Engaging Critical Thinking*. Upper Saddle River, NJ: Prentice-Hall.

Kerry, T. and Kerry, C (1997) 'Teaching the more able; primary and secondary practice compared', *Education Today*, 47: 11–16.

Koshy, V. (2001) *Teaching Mathematics to Able Children*. London: Fulton.

Koshy, V. and Casey, R. (2000) *Special Abilities Scales*. London: Hodder & Stoughton.

Leyden, S. (1998) *Supporting the Child of Exceptional Ability*. London: Fulton.

Maoz, N. (1993) 'Nurturing giftedness in non-school educative settings – using the personnel and material resources of the community', in K.A. Heller, F.J. Monks and A.H. Passow (eds) *International Handbook of Research and Development of Giftedness and Talent*. Oxford: Pergamon Press.

Marland, S.P. (1972) *Education of the Gifted and Talented. Report to the Congress of the United States by the U.S. Commissioner of Education*. Washington, DC: U.S. Government Printing Office.

Montgomery, D. (1996) *Educating the Very Able*. London: Cassell.

Montgomery, D. (2000) *Able Underachievers*. London Whurr.

Nisbet, J. (1990) 'Teaching thinking: an introduction to the research literature', *SCER Spotlight* No. 26.

Raven, J.C. (1938) *Raven's Progressive Matrices and Vocabulary Scales 8–14 Years*. Windsor: NFER Nelson.

Renzulli, J.S. (1995) 'New directions for the schoolwide enrichment model', in M.W. Katzko and F.J. Monks (eds) *Nurturing Talent; Individual Needs and Social Ability*. Assen, The Netherlands: Van Gorcum.

Rothman, G.R. (1992) 'Moral reasoning, moral behaviour, and moral giftedness: a developmental perspective', in Pnina S. Klein and A.J. Tannenbaum (eds) *To Be Young and Gifted*. New Jersey: Ablex.

Sheblanova, H. (1966) 'A longitudinal study of intellectual and creative development in gifted primary school children', *High Ability Studies*, 7: 51–4.

Shore, B.M. (2000) 'Metacognition and flexibility: qualitative differences in how gifted children think', in R.C. Friedman and B.M. Shore (eds) *Talents Unfolding: Cognition and Development.* Washington, DC: American Psychological Association.

Shore, B.M. and Delcourt, M.A.B. (1996) 'Effective curricular and program practices in gifted education and the interface with general education', *Journal for the Education of the Gifted*, 20: 138–54.

Shore, B.M., Cornell, D.G., Robinson, A. and Ward, V.S. (1991) *Recommended Practices in Gifted Education: A Critical Analysis.* New York: Teacher's College Press.

Sloboda, J. (1993) 'Musical ability', in G.R. Bock and K.A. Ackrill (eds) *The Origins and Development of High Ability* (Ciba Foundation Symposium). Chichester: Wiley.

Southern, W.T. and Jones, E.D. (eds) (1991) *The Academic Acceleration of Gifted Children.* New York: Teacher's College Press.

Span, P. (1995) 'Self-regulated learning by highly able children', in J. Freeman, P. Span and H. Wagner (eds) *Actualising Talent: a Lifelong Challenge.* London: Cassell.

Sternberg, R.J. (1985) *Beyond IQ: a Triarchic Theory of Human Intelligence.* Cambridge: Cambridge University Press.

Sternberg, R.J. (1993) 'Procedures for identifying intellectual potential in the gifted: a perspective on alternative "metaphors of mind"', in K.A. Heller, F.J. Monks and A.H. Passow (eds) *International Handbook of Research and Development of Giftedness and Talent.* Oxford: Pergamon Press.

Sternberg, R.J. (1997) 'Educating intelligence: infusing the Triarchic Theory into school instruction', in R.J. Sternberg and E. Grigorenko (eds) *Intelligence, Heredity and Environment.* Cambridge: Cambridge University Press.

Sternberg, R.J. (2007) *Wisdom, Intelligence, and Creativity Synthesized.* Cambridge: Cambridge University Press.

Sternberg, R. and Grigorenko, E. (1997) *Intelligence, Heredity and Environment.* Cambridge: Cambridge University Press.

Sternberg, R.J. and Lubart, T.I. (1995) *Defying the Crowd: Cultivating Creativity in a Culture of Conformity.* New York: Free Press.

Stopper, M.J. (2000) *Meeting the Social and Emotional Needs of Gifted and Talented Children.* London: Fulton.

Tempest, N.R. (1974) *Teaching Clever Children 7–11.* London: Routledge and Kegan Paul.

Torrance, E.P. (1987) 'Teaching for creativity' in S.G. Isaksen (ed.) *Frontiers of Creativity Research.* Buffalo, NY: Bearly.

Treffinger, D.J. and Feldhusen, J.F. (1996) 'Talent recognition and development: successor to gifted education', *Journal for the Education of the Gifted*, 19: 181–93.

Urban, K.K. (1995) 'Different models in describing, exploring, explaining and nurturing creativity in society', *European Journal for High Ability*, 6: 143–59.

Wagner, H. (1995) 'Non-school provision for talent development', in J. Freeman, P. Span and H. Wagner (eds) *Actualizing Talent: a Lifelong Challenge.* London: Cassell.

Walberg, H.J. (1995) 'Nurturing children for adult success', in M.W. Katzko and F.J. Monks (eds) *Nurturing Talent: Individual Needs and Social Ability.* Assen, The Netherlands: Van Gorcum.

Wallace, B. (2000) *Teaching the Very Able Child.* London: David Fulton.

Wallace, B. and Adams, H.B. (eds) (1993) *Worldwide Perspectives on the Gifted Disadvantaged.* Bicester: AB Academic Publishers.

West-Burnham, J. and Coates, M. (2005) *Personalizing Learning.* London: Network Education Press.

Winner, E. (1996) *Gifted Children: Myths and Realities.* New York: Basic Books.

Zha, Z. (1995a) 'Development of research and education of gifted children in China', paper given in Beijing, China, August.

Zha, Z. (1995b) 'The influence of family education on gifted children', paper presented at World Conference on Gifted and Talented Children, Hong Kong.

Index